Contents

CW00502314

The Message.

What quality sets man apart?
From the teeming, rich diversity,
Of species, which inhabit this,
Great planet, with its glistening seas,
Dense forests, under brazen skies,
Where creatures, fierce, and wild, and strange,
Eat and are eaten, live and die,
And learn, yes, but they never change.

They have, it seems, reached journey's end,
I mean in terms of evolution,
They are content with what they have,
For them, there'll be no revolution.
Naturalists have claimed, and will attest,
"The opposing thumb gave man the spur,"
Lemurs have that. Surely you jest!
They're just bewildered blobs of fur!

"The ability to stand erect,
Leaving, of course, your two hands free"
Like gorillas can? With due respect,
Try as I might, I just can't see,
Them taking over, driving cars,
Or building big, palatial homes,
Knocking it back, in cocktail bars,
While talking on their mobile phones.

Yes! That is the secret of success,
To form in clans, and tribes, and nations,
Not bigger muscles, longer necks,
The secret, is communication,
And you know, we have that in spades,
That is what has given us such clout,
Such nuances, such subtle shades,
Of meaning, have marked mankind out,

With just a few inspiring words,
Some men have changed the world, no question,
For those on the receiving end,
Are always open to suggestion,
I don't mean truth, although you'll find,
It helps, if you at least seem wise,
Most of the drivers of mankind,
Were built on well-constructed lies.

New fears for old.

In the old town where I was born,
Under a stand of doleful trees,
A dark house stood, in moss grown lawns,
Silent as ancient cemeteries,
Whenever I would pass the place,
I always had to look behind,
To where those black windows stared their hate,
Or sorrow, from the tangled vine.

But when five years had come and gone,
I knew my childish fantasies,
Had conjured ghouls, where there were none,
Grim visions of malignancy.
At fifteen now, and almost grown
My fevered brain teemed with the new,
Dark fantasies I would not own,
When Dad said, "I've a job for you,

For the old biddy up the lane,
Just tidying up her paths, and lawns,"
Then I would not refuse, for shame,
Dismissed the furtive chill with scorn.
But that first day I worked alone,
Under a massive, creaking yew,
For that strange thing of skin and bone,
Cut off, it seemed, from all I knew,

Standing like old clothes, at the door,
As I scraped rotting leaf-mould up,
She called me, with a beckoning claw,
To drink some fluid from a cup,
In, through a dim and musty hall,
Her drab form, limping on ahead,
Her tangled mass of hair, a ball,
Of old grey cobwebs, round her head.

Into a room, that reeked of time,
And dust, and age, and poverty,
She turned her creased-putty face to mine,
And sat me down, to wait for tea,
But, left alone, I gazed enthralled,
Where sunlight, through a dusty pane,
Fell on a portrait, on the wall,
Too golden for its gilded frame,

A lovely girl, whose limpid eyes,
Lit with a gentle inner glow,
Had looked on some quiet paradise,
And secrets only she could know,
Curved, in a smile of innocence,
Her tender mouth, and moved me so,
I knew, I would have no defence,
To that defenceless cupid's bow.

But when the shrivelled creature came,
Rattling her china, on a tray,
I looked, and looked away in shame,
Turning my guilty face away,
From what I saw, in those dark eyes,
Half lost, in convoluted folds,
I seemed to hear a querulous cry,
So faint and high, "New fears for old."

The shape of things.

Drab shades of the dead city crept my way,
As waning sunlight measured off the day,
A sudden movement, in the silent street,
The stealthy whisper of his alien feet.

This loathsome creature this vile world bad bred,
And then, above the stones, his fearsome head,
Across the littered street he ran, pell-mell,
Screaming in fear, my gun blazed, and he fell.

I stood, and looked at this thing I had killed,
Even though safe and dead, my blood was chilled,
This, the last beast of a most beastly race,
No horns or scales, adorned its pallid face

Only four limbs, all withered now, and grey,
I shuddered, as I turned, and walked away
And eyes, which had stood out on stalks with dread,
All slithered, slowly, back into my head.

Martyn of Mandeville

One.

If you would hear a tale, not of the world we Know,
If you would hear a romance of another day,
Come with me, and together we will go,
Back to a land of long ago, and far away,
To Martyn, son of Anselm, Duke of Mandeville,
Returning from his sojourn in a distant land,
Strong in the strength of learning (His great father's will)
Strong in the joy of youth, a boy become a man.

He'd slept beneath a willow tree,
Which drooped beside a crystal pool,
And now lay, pensive, in the cool,
Thinking that this day, he would see,
 Those loved ones who, when life was cruel,
Had cheered him with warm memories.

Anselm, his father, justly famed,
He who had won back this great land,
Fighting the tyrant, hand to hand,
Who'd held the common folk enchained,
Beneath his banner did they stand,
Freedom, and commonweal proclaimed.

Well had the great Duke ruled the land,
From the high mountains to the sea,
Setting all serfs and vassals free,
Fierce warriors knelt to kiss his hand
Pledging to him their fealty,
And to his wife, fair Alysande.

Beyond the mountains, blue and grey,
The northern point of the great plain,
Barbarian kings and princes reigned,
Vile cannibals, and folks did say,
Dragons and monsters, wild and strange,
Carried the little ones away.

Out to the West, green foothills lie,
Where goatherds ran their bleating flocks,
A mighty ridge of blackened rocks,
 Rose, sinister, against the sky,
Strange beasts would shake their shaggy locks,
At night, with many an eldritch cry.

But to the East, the sparkling sea,
Where cheerful fishers plied their trade,
And in those sturdy boats they made,
Lived in the joy of men made free,
For even when they worked, they played,
They lived, and loved, right merrily.

So all across this golden land,
Me revelled in the joy of life,
And to the gods, made sacrifice,
In honour of the noble man,
Who had made an end to bitter strife,
And held their welfare in his hand.

He thought of gentle Damaris,
The sweetheart of his childhood days,
Of all her tender winning ways,
Remembering their parting kiss,
And in her dark eye's tear-dimmed gaze,
Vague promises of future bliss.

Then Martyn stretched hid long-limbed frame,
Throwing his sleeping robe aside,
Stood naked, at the water side,
And plunging in, to cool the flame,
Thinking of she who would be his bride,
He turned his toilet to a game.

At length, awakened, and refreshed,
He got him from the sparkling pool,
A mossy boulder for a stool,
As speedily, he dried and dressed
The huge bay, grazing in the cool,
Came eagerly, at his behest.

So as the sun's first level rays,
Struck through the pale green willow stems,
Turning dew drops to glittering gems,
The man, and the high-stepping bay,
Those two well tried and trusted friends,
Followed their winding northward way.

As they traversed the valley side,
The young man's mind traversed the past,
And though this world is wide and vast,
He'd often dreamed this joyous ride,
Back to his father's home at last,
Through this familiar countryside.

He had been sent, a callow youth,
Tol learn what only life can teach,
to strive for heights beyond his reach,
And winning, losing find what truths,
The heart and mind can glean from each,
And he had learned full well, in sooth.

Had learned of politics, and law,
Of how the two go hand in hand,
For one day, he would rule this land,
His father said, "I must be sure,
My people's future will be planned,
Their health and welfare catered for."

He'd learned of war, and strategy,
The sacred duty of command,
And how to utilize the land,
To make best use of weaponry,
Vanquished his tutors, to a man,
So great had been his mastery.

Five years gone, and the slender lad,
Who first began that long sojourn,
Had grown a man, in beef and brawn,
Such height, and breadth, and strength he had,
It was his grandfather reborn,
He who was slain by Balthazad.

Two.

Some men see power as a sacred trust,
Such men are rare indeed, exceptions to the rule,
Most seek for power dissembling, with a secret lust,
And once attained, will use it as a tool,
Just such a man was Balthazad, of Wolvendale,
Beyond black mountains to the North of Mandeville
Fear stalked the land he ruled with a fist of mail,
And the eager swords of men who lived to do his will.

For it was said, he came in might,
The tyrant prince of his domain,
Where ere he ruled was fear and pain,
They came like foul thieves in the night,
Riding with Death across the plain,
And evil was the people's plight.

Stormed the great house of Walkindire,
The faithful servants to the sword,
His wife and daughter foully gored,
The ancient house their funeral pyre,
The great man stood against the horde,
The carnage that he wrought was dire.

His mighty sword-arm cut a swathe,
Scattered the murderous crew like chaff,
They say he gave an awful laugh,
Said, "Balthazad, for you, the grave,
I will cleave your evil heart in half"
Once more, into the press he drave.

But then the jackals pulled him down,
The blood- soaked sword slipped from his grasp,
And with a last, despairing gasp,
He plunged, defeated, to the ground,
Finding their courage at the last,
The bloody murderers gathered round.

The house in flames, his family dead,
All save the one, tall Martyn's sire,
For when they perished in the pyre,
Anselm was lying, safe abed,
In a far city, and the fire,
Threw capering shadows around his head,

As he slept on, and dreamed, he saw,
A black- haired tyrant, steeped in sin,
The evil murder of his kin,
Cried out, and waking, knew for sure,
The awful vision he had seen,
Was very truth and slept no more.

And long before the chilly dawn,
Young Anselm, pale, and sick at heart,
Had made that weary journey's start,
Rode through the drab and misty morn,
Hoping on hope it would depart,
This vision which had made him mourn.

But when the young man came at last,
Back to the country of his birth,
And saw the scarred and fire scorched earth,
Then he reined in, and stood aghast,
He thought his life of little worth,
And scorching tears came thick and fast

The old hamlets and villages,
Were smoking ruins in the glens,
And blackened things that had been men,
Hung grim and stark from wayside trees,
Such evil things did he see then,
He never more would know true ease.

And then, alas, as he rode in,
From secret places in the wood,
People he knew, honest and good,
Came to him, hollow eyed and thin,
Telling how Balthazad, man of blood,
Outdid his brutal men in sin.

Of Athelstan, his general,
Who followed where his master led,
A handsome man, whose hands were red,
With blood of maids, taken in thrall,
And innocents, untimely dead
Yet stood, and gently smiled withal,

While his marauders fired the wheat,
And slaughtered all the sheep and goats,
Wantonly cut the poor beast's throats,
For sport, and when they were replete,
Destroyed the goodly stores of oats,
Leaving the people nought to eat.

One weeping ancient told Anselm,
A tale that struck him to the heart,
Of his fair household torn apart,
His mighty father overwhelmed.
Balthazad, by his evil art,
Now ruled over his father' realm
.

But when they told him how the death,
Of dam and sister came to pass,
He fell, insensate, in the grass,
Sweet Alysande breathed him her breath,
Lips on his lips, the tender lass,
Brought Anselm from the jaws of death

For two long years, a beast at bay,
An outlaw, in his father' land,
He gathered and armed a motley band,
Harried his foemen, made them pay,
And every waking hour, he planned,
His vengeance for that hateful day.

At last, the judgement day arrived,
They took Balthazad's hall by storm,
Men rued the day that they were born,
The murderers begged him for their lives,
Said Anselm, "Loved ones we all mourn,
Not one of you escapes alive!"

Anselm looked in Balthazad's face,
And after all those grievous times,
Said, "Now you answer for your crimes,
In this good land you have debased,
For with my father's sword, now mine,
I will give you death for your dis-grace."

"In very truth," Cried Balthazad,
I was the death of all your kin,
You will share with them the grave they're in,
And then he laughed as one gone mad,
His wild eyes flashing, black as sin,
He drew the long black sword he had.

In parrying the wild thrusts he made,
The great swords rang from point to hilt,
Then in atonement for his guilt
The tyrant took his victim's blade,
At last, his own foul blood was spilt,
Some part of his soul's debt was paid.

His brutal henchmen to the sword,
And after justice had been done,
Young Rodolfo, the tyrant's son,
Was found, concealed beneath a board,
 Anselm said, "take this little one,
Back to his home. That is my word."

Three.

Martyn thought of times before his birth,
Of Walkindire the Strong, his own grandsire,
Beset by Balthazad of Wolvendale,
He thought of Mandeville put to the fire,
His Father Anselm, as he did today,
Riding home from long years, in a far- off land,
To find the land of childhood in a tyrant's hands.

Yet this had happened long ago,
Before young Martyn had been born,
But now, on this propitious morn,
He viewed the valley, far below,
With fat sheep grazing, newly shorn,
Beside the silver river's flow.

From hamlets in the lingering mist,
The early morning sounds arose,
The bark of dogs, and shrill cock crows,
 And where the morning sunshine kissed,
The ancient walls were turned to rose,
In that fair valley, so long missed,

And when at length, the stately steed,
Paced down the old well-trodden ways,
Children came, open mouthed, to gaze,
Saying, "This must be a god indeed,"
His flaxen hair, in the sun's rays,
Hung, like a halo, round his head.

But when their fathers came to see,
The handsome youth astride the bay,
One to another did they say,
"The son of he who set us free,
Is back among us this great day."
And bonny maidens bent the knee.

Then, through the trees upon the hill,
The house his father had re-built,
He dashed his tears away with guilt,
Reined in the horse, and looked his fill,
Then, smiling through the tears he'd spilt,
Crossed the great bridge to Mandeville,

When he saw Martyn on the way,
Anselm had felt a sudden chill,
Thinking his own sire came, until,
He heard the whinny of the bay,
For joy to be at Mandeville,
Then he stood, wiping tears away.

The two men met upon the lawn,
And all the weary times were gone,
Tall Anselm, and his taller son,
Who to an outlaw had been born,
For so long parted, once more one,
Stood in embrace that golden morn.

Came Alysande, that beauteous dame,
Who gave him, and his father life,
Was loving mother, faithful wife,
And gave to both these roles the same,
Honesty, love, and sacrifice.
Kissed and embraced, then kissed again,

Then looked upon him, hard and long,
From booted feet to golden head,
"What alchemy is this?" She said,
"For I have lost my little one,
And find a giant in his stead,
Kiss me again, my long- lost son."

Now anxious Martyn looked in vain,
For Damaris, of whom he'd dreamed,
Such dreams of longing, when it seemed,
He would never see her face again,
Or those dark, gentle eyes, that gleamed,
With unshed tears, at parting's pain,

When Martyn first beheld the maid,
In all her womanly loveliness,
Saw how her sweet dark eyes confessed,
And all her tender love betrayed,
He knew himself a man so blessed,
That suddenly, he was afraid,

That sometimes, gifts the gods bestow,
The gods will take away again,
Peace turn to war, pleasure to pain,
"Come to me gentle maid, I vow,
That we shall never part, us twain,
Henceforth, where I go, you shall go."

What jubilation that fine day,
In the great house at Mandeville,
Nobles and peasants climbed the hill,
Caroused, and danced the night away,
And each, and every, drank his fill,
In honour of their wedding day.

What precious days, and how they flew,
For Martyn, and his comely bride,
They rode the valleys, far and wide,
Or lay and dreamed, as lovers do,
Sat fishing at the riverside,
And every day, their great love grew.

But the strange forebodings Martyn knew,
Returned when gentle Damaris,
Greeting him, as ever, with a kiss,
Said," Love, your father waits for you,
To meet him beneath the obelisk,
In memory of the loved ones who,

Fell at the hands of Balthazad,"
That instant Martyn knew for sure,
The fearful time he'd waited for,
Was here. He strode out, strangely sad,
To see what the fates had in store,
And face it with what strength he had.

His father waited, white as bone,
So quietly, he spoke his name,
Troubled, and with a look of shame,
"Martyn, I speak to you alone,
I fear I may have lived in vain,
My heart is heavy as this stone."

"I freed Rodolfo long ago,
Before you saw the light of day,
And sent him and his dam away,
I dreamed the mighty gods would show,
The evil of his father's ways,
But good cannot from evil grow."

"It seems the years have hurried by,
Rodolfo is a powerful man,
He has raised an army in his land,
To see his father's killers die,
Exact the vengeance, so long planned."
Bright tears stood in his father's eyes.

"Martyn, I do not fear to die,
Or the god's judgement on my life,
If it is my fate to die in strife,
But I still hear my people cry,
Upon the vile Balthazad's knife,
I feel his evil drawing nigh."

So, for my well- loved people's sake,
I must ask my more loved son,
For, Martyn, you're the only one,
Though I fear that my heart will break,
To do this thing, which must be done,
Gamble for peace, your life the stake."

He held his son then, in his arms,
A mighty shudder shook his frame,
But then he was himself again,
An ancient scroll, hung round with charms,
Much scorched by some long burned -out flame,
Bearing his great grandfather's arms,

Was spread, with care, upon the sward,
His father's finger traced the lines,
And faded, long forgotten signs,
Penned perhaps, by some long dead bard,
Speaking of wizards and divines,
And of an ancient godling's sword.

And after this, a simple plan,
"For years, I've dreamed of this," he said,
As Martyn sadly shook his head,
"For it is written here, the man,
Who owned that mighty weapon, led,
His people to a golden land."

"This is the land of which it speaks,
And somewhere, that great sword still lies,
Hidden for years from human eyes,
Near one of those black mountain peaks,
Where, in ages gone, that leader died,
Who finds the sword finds all he seeks."

"My father, this is not the way,
If war must come to this our land,
Be sure, your son is not the man,
Who willingly would ride away,
On some wild dream, or fool's errand,
If we must fight, then let me stay."

Anselm said ,"Do this son, for me,
For all we know, it may be true,
Our future may depend on you,
But if proud Rodolfo you should see,
Then number well his evil crew,
And bring the news back home to me."

When tearful Damaris was told,
She held him fiercely to her breast,
But she was equal to the test,
Saying, with a look, level and bold,
"Before our union was blessed,
You made a vow. Does it still hold?"

The lovers rode out at midnight,
Turning them northward, in the dark,
In silence through Mandeville Park,
Beneath the hood, her eyes were bright,
 Under the old trees, cold and stark,
Her loving heart was warm and light.

For days they rode, through sun and rain,
Past barren rocks and flowered fields,
And every passing day revealed,
To Martyn, what, with love, he had gained,
And what a harvest love can yield.
At last, they came to the great plain.

Across the wind- blown plain, they saw,
The mountains, black against the sky,
Beneath a massive tree did lie,
To watch the red sun sink once more,
Then, in the dark, he heard her sigh,
He never knew such love before,

For many days they crossed the plain,
A wilderness, a trackless waste,
When evening fell, they cleared a space,
To light a fire, and not in vain,
Wild beasts got them away in haste,
In fear of the bright, crackling flames.

They came at length, to rising ground,
Where neither trees nor grasses grew,
But jagged boulders, grey and blue,
Huge, echoing caves, and all around,
A never- ending wind, that blew,
Among the rocks, with hateful sounds,

As though some dying creature moaned,
From some uncanny, gaping maw,
And in the darkest caves, they saw,
Great shaggy beasts, who sadly groaned,
And watched them mournfully, before,
They disappeared, into the ground.

But soon they left this eerie place,
Hitting upon a mountain trail,
And here, the wind became a gale,
Until, beneath a tall cliff-face,
They made their camp upon the shale,
And took the old map from its case.

For on the pathway, far ahead,
There loomed a strange, misshapen stone,
As though a mighty tree had grown,
And stood there still, though it was dead,
Its ancient timbers turned to bone,
Rigid and white, a thing of dread.

And Martyn, when he spied the tree,
Knew the old map had led them true,
Their weary journey almost through,
He showed the tattered scroll to she,
Who had been his helpmeet, good and true,
And would, he prayed, forever be.

But then they heard a strange, shrill cry,
A shaggy man-thing, far below,
Released some missile from a bow,
And Martyn saw the arrow fly,
His fair Damaris took the blow,
And sighing, in his arms did lie.

He laid her gently on the shale,
The arrow shaft beneath her breast,
Her precious life blood soaked her dress,
Her lovely face so ghastly pale,
Her breathing shallow and distressed,
Then Martyn feared her heart would fail.

He pulled the crude shaft from her flesh,
  Binding her hurt, as best he could,
  Cried out against the gods who would,
  Make sport of mortal man's distress,
  He heard her whisper, "Hush my love,
  For to this day, I have been blessed

"The gods will keep me at your side,
  Until your father's quest is done,
  And if in truth, my race is run,
  Take heart, my love, I was the bride,
  To one of all beneath the sun,
  No other man could stand beside."

Then Martyn kissed her ashen face,
  And though his tears would not abate,
  He knelt, and prayed for his sweet mate,
  Thinking, "If there is a god of grace,
  If this must be my true love's fate,
  Then let me die in this grim place."

But then, among the rocks, hard by,
  A rattling hail of arrows fell,
  Again, that hateful. Bubbling yell,
  He stood, and there arose a cry,
  A fearsome sound, and he knew well,
  He and his bride were like to die.

He had heard, in tales of old,
That living in these mountains then,
Were eldritch beasts, beyond his ken,
Grey ghouls, who guarded hoards of gold,
And men who ate the flesh of men,
Then Martyn felt his blood run cold.

Standing a moment in full view,
And reaching down his hunting bow,
He saw the rabblement below,
Come on apace, with fierce halloo,
Then Martyn let his arrows go,
And now the hellish clamour grew.

Screaming their hate at every stride,
They came on, over rocks and scree,
And Martyn suddenly could see,
A way to stem the deadly tide,
He heaved a massive boulder free,
To roll on down the mountain side.

Now cries of fear rose from the pack,
As Martyn hurled the boulders down,
A trembling shook the very ground,
The dust pall turned the sky to black,
A darkness filled with dreadful sounds,
And the mountain shook them from its back,

As water, shaken from a hound,
The harsh wind bore away the pall,
And silence settled over all,
Then Martyn, trembling, looked around,
Where dark eyes watching, still and small,
Pale Damaris lay on the ground.

A thicket of green aspen trees,
Grew, stunted, on the small plateau,
Martyn took his sword and bow,
To cut and trim the best of these,
And make a litter he could tow,
Behind the bay, for his love's ease.

So thus, they came to the strange tree,
Of gleaming white, like sun bleached bone,
A huge cave, and a slab of stone,
His sturdy sword would be the key,
Driven in a crevice, with a moan,
The ancient granite slab slid free.

And in a hollow, something lay,
Wrapped all around in faded skins,
As Martyn reached his two hands in,
He felt at once afraid, and fey,
That it may be a mortal sin,
To take this aged thing away.

But then, lifted the bundle out,
And took the thing to Damaris,
"My love," He said, "You must see this,"
Pulling at the dry skins wrapped about,
Which clung, as though they would resist,
At last, he drew his broadsword out.

With the good sword, he made a stroke,
The keen edged blade sank through the skins,
An awful sound came from within,
The broad blade, scorched, and black with smoke,
This sword his sire had given him,
Fell from his nerveless hand, and broke,

In blackened shards upon the sward,
Bur Martyn grimly clenched his teeth,
Against his weakness, fear, and grief,
Remembering his father's word,
He pulled aside the withered sheath,
And saw the mighty godling's sword.

It seemed the sword leapt to his hand,
To nestle in his finger's clutch,
And there was something in that touch,
That somehow, he could understand,
Here was a sword that only such,
As he could ever take in hand.

He took and laid his gentle wife,
Behind a stand of twisted trees,
Laid her secure, and on his knees,
Prayed to the gods, for her sweet life,
She whispered, "Love, I am at ease,
Just leave me water, and a knife."

He stumbled back into the cave,
Into a cavern, ages old,
Deep into darkness, and to cold,
The sputtering sparks his bright torch gave,
Fell, hissing, in the ooze and mould,
In that fell place, cold as the grave.

Labyrinthine tunnels, echoing,
With whispers of another time,
And dim-seen beasts, carved in the grime,
And all around, the sound of things,
That shuffled with him, through the slime,
Or fluttered by, on leathern wings.

From darkness to a mighty chamber,
Bright with phosphorescent light,
Some fearsome creature of the night,
Got to its scaly legs and came,
Its great maw yawned to rend and bite,
Its taloned claws outstretched to maim.

The beast's eyes held him in its thrall,
A choking breath caught in his throat,
As rabbits freeze before a stoat,
He shrank against the cavern's wall,
The sword vibrated with a note,
That rang out, like a clarion call.

The great sword sang against his thigh,
His mighty sword arm rose and fell,
Sending the creature back to Hell,
The light went from its yellow eyes,
As with a whistling roar, it fell,
Into the ooze and mire to die.

At the foul cavern's furthest wall,
A narrow arch, where faint light gleamed,
And feeling that he surely dreamed,
He stepped into a carven hall,
A place so huge and vast, it seemed,
The roof could not be seen at all.

And in the centre, on a stage,
A tall, pale, shimmering figure stood,
Half seen, half unseen, Martyn could,
Feel in this soul of some past age,
A sense of power, and of good,
He stood, afraid, before the mage.

The figure held a golden grail,
And in a far-off voice, he said,
"Thou standest, Martyn, in my stead,
Take thou the chalice, do not fail,
For thou hast earned it, heart and head.
And get thee back to thy travail."

He reached, and took the golden bowl,
From one who had died in ages gone,
And in its depth, he saw the sun,
Burning with fires that seared his soul,
The great earth spinning, spinning on,
Through all the long- lost times of old.

Though in his heart, he feared the sight,
He gazed into the brimming bowl,
Saw purple, amber, liquid gold,
Vermilion, scarlet, shards of light,
Rose from some unfathomable hole,
To burst, like bright stars in the night.

He drank the seething liquid down,
And felt a fire surge through his veins,
Somewhere, he heard a cry of pain,
The chamber wildly spun around,
He stared into the bowl again,
As though he would plunge in and drown.

Saw through the awful void of time,
Vast swamps, beneath a brassy sky,
Great creatures live, and fight, and die,
Strange fruits and flowers, and in his mind,
He saw the ages passing by,
In fragrance of lost summer times.

The smiling mage gave him a bow,
Then faded, with a silent wave,
And now the great hall was a cave,
The bright light dwindled to a glow,
A blast of air, as from the grave,
And Martyn quickly turned to go.

The ante- chamber dim and bare,
The baleful thing he'd killed, was gone,
Chilled to the bone, he hurried on,
Through passages that seemed aware,
At last, the light of blessed sun,
He staggered into open air.

A dread fear held him in its grip,
As he came to where Damaris lay,
So still, so pale, yet did she pray,
"Let not my own dear Martin slip,
Bring him back safe to me this day,"
He held the chalice to her lip.

Four.

They rode on, down the mountain way,
Left far behind, the tree of bone,
His sweet love's fever was all gone,
And teasing coquettish and gay,
Or laughing, singing, in the sun,
She warmed his troubled heart with play.

When he gave Damaris the draught,
She lay, faintly breathing, at his side,
And sometimes, in the night, she cried,
Sometimes she spoke, and softly laughed,
With dawn's first light, she awoke, great eyed,
Said, "Martyn, I have seen such craft,

So many wonders I have seen,
That I shall never fear again."
And oh, my love, I have no pain,
Come, let us leave this place of dreams,
And get us to our home again,
My heart cries out for fields of green."

At length, they crossed the wilderness,
Came to a pool, ringed around with trees,
Here, for a time, they took their ease,
They swam and played in thankfulness,
And Martyn, wondering, could see,
No arrow mark beneath her breast.

But when they left this place of flowers,
They saw the marks of many hooves,
And in the softer ground, deep grooves,
They followed through the morning hours,
Martyn said, "My love, I fear this proves,
Black Rodolfo, and all his powers,

Are massing now, for the attack,
Great ordnance has passed this way,
And that, I think, within a day,
To do my duty, never lack,
To the all -seeing gods I pray,
For we are hard upon his back"

They reached a place where blackthorns grew,
Twixt huge rocks on the steep hillside.
And now the two made shift to hide,
For in the valley, just below,
Filling the vale from side to side,
The armies of Black Rodolfo.

Searching along the valley side,
Among the rocks, and flowering trees,
To lie secure from enemies
They found a cave, shallow, and wide
He kissed her then, said, "Be at ease,
I shall return at eventide."

They led the mounts into the cave,
Concealed it with a fallen tree,
"Oh Martyn, now I fear for thee,"
Cried Damaris, "I will be brave,
But oh, my love, come back to me,
To kiss again your little slave,"

Through tumbled rocks, and twisted pine,
On foot he went, from East to West,
Keeping ever below the crest,
Till, coming to a steep incline,
He crawled beneath a bush to rest,
And found the entrance to a mine.

Two uprights and a lintel stone,
grown all around with foliage,
The moss- grown stone fissured with age,
Yet in the shaft, a faint light shone,
And in his mind, it seemed, the mage,
Said "Forward Martyn, get thee on,"

And once inside the shaft, he saw,
A faint fluorescence all around,
And up ahead, a roaring sound,
As distant waves upon a shore,
He knew somehow, this place he'd found,
Was one he had known, years before.

The tunnel, hewn through rock and shale,
Was driven deep into the hill,
Ascending ever more, until,
Cursing time lost to no avail,
The faint glow growing brighter still,
Martyn stepped out, into a gale.

He stood upon a towering tor,
And all around him, ancient spoil,
Coarse grass grew in the flinty soil,
With flowering gorse, and hellebore,
Bright heathers, broom, and cinquefoil,
Then Martyn gazed around in awe.

Full fifty strides across the green,
A wall of tall stones, where a man,
Could stand erect, and yet command,
All things below, and not be seen,
Through narrow slots, he viewed the land,
Below, as one fast in a dream.

He watched then, through this man-made crack,
As down upon the valley floor,
The enemy prepared for war,
A flaunting pennant, red and black,
He knew that moment that he saw,
The lord Rodolfo's bivouac.

Five.

Damaris sat beneath the tree,
And prayed for Martyn's safe return,
Doubting and hoping, turn by turn,
She heard his footfalls in the scree,
The loved form her prayers had earned,
And the gentle lady's tears flowed free.

He told her then of what he had found,
"But we cannot leave the mounts behind,
For the lord Rodolfo's men to find."
"Martyn, the pool with willows round,
It's just a little way behind,
Surely there they won't be found."

When Damaris first saw the place,
"Oh, god's above, I want to cry,
Who would build such a place, and why?
This surely is a site of grace,
It is like a garden in the sky."
And laughing, Martyn kissed her face.

The lovers then, with wondering eyes,
Explored the garden, hand in hand,
While Martyn told what he had planned,
"Within an easy bow shot, lies,
The bivouac of that vile man,
Yet I gain little if he dies."

"Beneath yon banner, black and red,
There will his generals meet, I think,
Eat their fine meat, drink their strong drink,
Prepare them for the fight ahead,
The one by one, away they'll slink,
Off to their pallets, and to bed,

Befuddled by the honeyed mead,
 Poured down their throats for courage's sake,
But first, each man a trip will take,
Into yon patch of scrub and weed,
Betwixt them and the little lake,
Men will not fight with none to lead."

Then for a time, the rugged crag,
Became a garden of delight,
The lovers, soulmates, man, and wife,
The gentle hind, the noble stag,
Each blessed the other, till the light,
Of westering sun began to flag,

Then in the valley, a brave show,
Rodolfo's generals round the fire,
Resplendent in their rich attire,
Posturing, swaggering to and fro,
Then, as the eager flames grew higher,
"Damaris, kiss me, I must go."

Beyond the red fire's hiss and crack,
The ever- darker shadows creep,
A grey- beard general thinks of sleep,
"Lord Rodolfo, I think I lack,
Or maybe I have drunk too deep,
I'll get me to my bivouac."

Then one by one, their thirst is slaked.
Fighting grim battles with their eyes,
They aid each other to arise,
And stumbling, staggering, half awake,
As Martyn stares in grim surprise,
Each one goes to his sleeping place.

Then, left alone, Lord Rodolfo,
Rises, unsteady, from his seat,
Fuddled with wine, and too replete,
Staggers to Martyn, halt and slow,
And Martyn, leaping to his feet,
Has felled him with a single blow!

Still, in the vale, faint embers gleam,
All else below is lost to sight,
An evil, black, and moonless night,
Then to pale Damaris, it seems,
That something creeping out of sight,
Some hateful thing of evil dreams,

Crawls ever closer in the gloom,
She hears the slither of its feet,
And then a voice, so passing sweet,
"Fair Damaris, am I too soon?
I bring to you a joint of meat,
A lover's offering from your groom."

And Martyn's gift sat on the ground,
When bright dawn paled the eastern sky,
Against a thorn bush, all awry,
Rodolfo, most securely bound,
With hate and murder in his eye,
And wildly staring all around.

But then came one, who bore a gourd,
And savoury morsels on white lace,
Removed the muffle from his face,
"Good day," He said, "To you, my lord,
I bid you welcome to this place,
Observe, I have your dag and sword."

Bent twixt Rodolfo and the post,
And both his captive's hands were free,
Rodolfo chafed them tenderly,
"It seems that I address my host,
Pray tell me what you want of me,
Be sure, you kill me at your cost."

"But if you plan to ransom me,
The I salute you on your plan,
Though clearly, you're a base brigand,
My people will pay handsomely,
And make of you a wealthy man,
For Lord Rodolfo, hale and free,"

And thus Rodolfo softly spoke,
His black eyes glittering hatefully,
"Come fellow, loose me from this tree,
I have such pain since I awoke,
And you have all the weaponry,
I cannot long endure this yoke."

"Be of good cheer," said Martyn then,
"And eat the victuals while you can,
All in good time, you'll hear my plan,
Be sure, you will have need of them,
To fortify the inner man,
For soon I will return again,"

But left alone, Rodolfo fought,
Striving amain against the knots,
The more he strove, the worse his lot,
So cunningly had they been wrought,
And sweating, cursing, tired and hot,
He ate the breakfast Martyn brought.

Six.

Martyn and Damaris embraced,
Under a group of standing stones,
Where some wild vine for years had grown,
Making a curtain round the place,
He whispered, "Keep you here my own,
And I will entertain his grace."

Martyn approached as though in play,
Saying, "Hail to thee, my potent lord,
Soon I will unloose that irksome cord,
But firstly, I have much to say,
And many things must be assured,
For this day is our judgement day,"

"For well I know you, Rodolfo,
Foul leader of an evil band,
Who threatens my good father's land,
As your own sire did, long years ago,
Now you shall learn what I have planned,
I sow the seeds, you make them grow."

"What arrant folly you dispense,
In truth, you are an addled churl,
Speaking in riddles, as a girl,
Speak not in vile Anselm's defence,
That man is not long for this world.
If you would talk with me, talk sense,"

"Then list to me, proud Rodolfo,
(And listen also, gods divine)
There is bad blood twixt thine and mine,
Yet of your people, there below,
Not one in ten knows aught of mine,
But for our quarrel, they will go,

To evil death, to blood and gore,
Defending your unholy creed,
You seek this battle, not from need,
But as your father did before,
You would stab, just to see men bleed,
And make war for the sake of war."

The Rodolfo threw back his head,
And laughed, as he would surely choke,
"In sooth, this is a telling joke,
Is this the man your land has bred,
How blessed are your women- folk,
Perhaps they fight us in your stead."

Martyn said, "Hear you now, my plan,
The war will be twixt you and me,
If you are victor, you go free,
A message, penned in my own hand,
Will bear news of your victory,
And by my word, my word will stand."

And only this I ask of you,
If you should best me in the fight,
The swear by all the gods of might,
That to this pledge you will be true,
To rule my much- loved land aright,
Matching the old rule with the new."

"But if it is the god's design,
And you are fated to be slain,
Your people go back, whence they came,
And never shall men of your line,
Make war on men of mine again,
What say you, to this plan of mine?"

"I say, this gamble pleases me,
To save your people from the rule,
Of one who is an arrant fool,
Cut me these irksome small cords free,
And give to me my weapon, fool,
 And we shall see what we shall see."

So, Martyn brought his writing case,
And when the black duke's pledge was made,
He smiled, and drew the shining blade,
Smiled in Rodolfo's ashen face,
And with a stroke, severed the braid,
Which held his enemy in place.

Seven.

Rodolfo got upon his knees,
And stared around as one in dread,
"What alchemy is this," he said,
I feel as one who has drunk the lees,
Or dined with ergot in the bread,"
"Calm you," Said Martyn, "Be at ease,

My lord, here is no alchemy,
We stand upon that towering tor,
Beneath, your host prepares for war,
Get on your legs, and you will see,
That here, I am the only law,
Prepare yourself for war, with me."

Then on the valley, far below,
Confused sounds of the waking brute,
Great generals stood irresolute,
One saying "Come," another "Go,"
What one proposed, one would refute,
They searched for the Lord Rodolfo.

My lord turned from the scene below,
Tall, dark, and slender, yet with power
"Come, let us fight among these flowers,
I shall not kill you with one blow,
He smiled, yet did his black eyes glower,
"Your death will be exceeding slow."

But Martyn, smiling at his word,
And in his eyes, an eager light,
Said, "If I have judged you aright,
You are no stranger to the sword,
Methinks we'll make a merry fight,
Take up your weapon, now, my lord."

Rodolfo plied his sword with flair,
A swordsman, this, of passing skill,
And drove at Martyn with a will,
His bright blade whistled through the air,
Each slashing blow to maim, or kill,
But Martyn's sword was always there.

The tramp of feet, the clashing blades,
The hot breath, burning in the breast,
Rodolfo now, was sorely pressed,
A ring of steel around him played,
His rival was a man possessed,
And suddenly he was afraid.

Then Martyn struck a mighty blow,
The sword flew from Rodolfo's hand,
Spun ringing through the air, to land,
Down in the bushes, far below,
The black Duke knew then he was damned,
And shuddering from head to toe,

He tore the doublet from his chest,
"Strike well, my hated enemy,
And set your foeman's spirit free,
For I will hate you to the last,
And all your evil family,
Come, make an end, my time is past."

But Martyn sheathed his blade again,
"I will not kill you, Rodolfo,
Your people follow where you go,
Our bargain would have been in vain,
Without your life, to make it so,
For you the loss, for me, no gain."

Then Rodolfo sat in the grass,
"What man is this, who strives and toils,
Winning the fight, takes not the spoils
Who talks in riddles, like an ass,
Yet traps Rodolfo in his coils,
I pray this evil dream will pass."

"You, from the loins of a lord,
Who foully murdered all my kin,
Whose very soul is black with sin,
Defeats a master of the sword,
Spirits me from ten thousand men,
How can we be of one accord?"

"I know you have no love for me,"
Said Martyn, "And I know you sought,
Vengeance for crimes my father wrought,
We are bound by our history,
But could it be, if we were taught,
A different tale, we could be free?"

"Rodolfo, history can lie,
 A story shifting as ' tis told,
Old heroes were forever bold,
Each for the right, would live or die,
And every maid was pure as gold,
Let us consider, you and I,

Where was your father, years ago,
When he fell, at my father's hand?
Then, at the mercy of this man,
And you an infant, I would know,
How came you back to your own land,
Out of the stronghold of your foe?"

The dark duke leapt then, to his feet,
"This son of Anselm has a tongue,
Ye gods, you make the right seem wrong,
If evil brings its own defeat,
Then right is ever with the strong.
Is there no end to your deceit?"

"This talk is wearisome and vain,
My pledge is made, my word is good,
But I would rather die in blood,
Than hear you black my father's name,
You are your father's son. You would,
Perjure your soul, to hide his shame."

Said Martyn, "You may call me knave,
But there's a greybeard in your host,
A man whose seen more years than most,
A tall, spare man, and very grave,
He is the one to lay this ghost,
Methinks he is a man, and brave."

"The one you speak of, Athelstan,
He has been mentor unto me,
Taught me the ways of chivalry,
In truth, I know no better man,
In wisdom, and sagacity,
How can he be part of your plan?"

"Tis by our faith we stand or fall,
Bring me this man, at eve of day,
And let no other see the way,
Nor let him know what will befall,
There is but one game left to play,
Then we both win, or both lose all."

Eight.

They watched the valley at their ease,
Saw Rodolfo, at eventide,
And saw one other, at his side,
Damaris whispered, "Martyn, please,
How do you know what will betide?
And learn to trust your enemies?"

Said Martyn, "Love, I'm only sure,
Of what is gone, not what's to come,
But we are outnumbered, five to one,
And if it ever comes to war,
My father will be overrun,
So peace is what I gamble for."

We are like fish, upon a line,
Running a course we think is planned,
Yet guided by some unseen hand,
And whether baleful or benign,
Is past our wit to understand,
And we shall only learn with time."

"But by Rodolfo's fire, last night,
I heard a name men speak with dread,
And saw a man I thought long dead,
It seems at last, the gods requite,
His blood, for all the blood he shed,
For all the lives he took, his life."

Deep shadows flood the valley floor,
Bright day is fading into night,
And moving through the dwindling light,
Among the trees below the tor,
The two below are lost to sight,
And the red sun is gone once more.

At last, they stood upon the rock,
"What trick is this!" Cried Athelstan,
"By the great gods, I knew this man,
In a past time," He reeled in shock.
The sword fell from his palsied hand,
"Now are the dead come back to mock."

"In faith, my very blood is cold,
This apparition turns my head,
What is this fell place of the dead?
Stand with me Rod, my tale is told.
My heart misgives me, all is dread,
And suddenly, I am grown old,"

"Why man, you blench, and shake with fear,
What so unmans you, Athelstan,
Long have I known you, boy and man,
And never saw you shed a tear,
Answer me truly, if you can,
Or this day you pay all arrears."

"Rodolfo, if I am to die,
Then I'll say what I have to say,
I knew your father, on a day,
And by his hand, my soul's awry,
The time's o'erpast for me to pay,
But let me not die with a lie."

"The fair land which you rule so well,
Your father Balthazad, ruled ill,
Bending the people to his will,
Making their lives a living Hell,
His evil soul affects me still,
We did such things; I could not tell.

I think Balthazad loved to kill,
There was some demon in his head,
I still remember it with dread,
The way we sacked poor Mandeville,
The sun shines brighter since he's dead,
Tomorrow, will shine brighter still."

He leapt then, from the towering tor,
Into the jagged rocks below,
Leaving the weeping Rodolfo,
"There was no man that I loved more,
The gods judge me this day, I vow,
My father, and my loved mentor,"

"Are lost to me in one fell stroke,
In faith, I am overcome with ruth,
An oft repeated lie my truth,
And all my life an evil joke."
But then, the old mage, speaking sooth,
Appeared, all wreathed about with smoke,

And icy crystals in the air,
"List unto me, thou grieving soul,
The gods from each, exact their toll,
The steeper way, the greater fare,
And if a man would reach his goal,
Soon or late, he must pay his share."

"Thou shalt repay thy father's debt
And save thy line from infamy,
Rule over happy men, and free,
Thy great land shall be greater yet,
And all shall bless thy memory,
When at long last, thy sun has set."

When bright dawn broke, over the vale,
Rodolfo's camp was all astir,
Damaris, wrapped in a great fur,
Seated with Martyn, on a bale
Said to Rodolfo, "Tell me, sir,
How is your life, in Wolvendale?"

"Damaris, Martyn, if you will,
Ride there with me, and you will find,
Small difference twixt your land and mine."
Said Martyn, "One day soon, but still,
Rodolfo, how our two hearts pine,
We ride, this day, for Mandeville,"

Esperanto for beginners.

Amma chugga, grun tsat rane,
Amma zu macri zap lane
Wotta miden astak ah
Uzar acer swa tuar
Mu derfat cowin dergrass
Atta mo tawi zinpast,
Wy latrac torin daf eeld
Rat eldow tabiz eereel
Bur nin gupda dese eloyl
Andap lout urndup Dassoyl
Forda cede atwas taccum
Nowat win tawaz aldun.

Links in the Food Chain.

I have a cat, a mouth on furry legs,
Rounded and plump, quite pleasing to the eye,
Ten times an hour, he rubs round me, and begs,
For food, and he has never been too shy,
(Although he bulges still, with what he ate,
For breakfast) to steal morsels from my plate.

It beats me, how a creature whose so small,
Though Bickie's fat enough, I must confess,
Can pack so much food away, then all,
The morning, whinge at me, a total pest.
Until at last, I have to give him more,
I wonder that his feet still reach the floor.

When not eating, or slobbing on the rug,
Or yowling at me, to be let in, or out,
To do his toilet, in the hole he's dug,
Scooting my newly planted bulbs about,
He creeps about the garden, in the sun,
Tearing the heads off little birds, for fun.

"But, it's in the nature of a cat, to kill,"
They say, "It shows his spirit is still free."
That may be so, last week, when I was ill,
I did not like the way he looked at me.
Now, I fear, that same look is in my eye,
I wonder what he'd taste like, in a pie.

A Bedtime Fable.

How they were feted, those great men,
We shall never see their like again,
The headline said "Ten out of Ten,"
A telling phrase.
Ten life-forms, changed genetically,
All humankind at last set free,
From sickness, and from drudgery,
So the paper says.

Three of the team had died, we learned,
Two more of them were badly burned,
How richly had those great men earned,
Their Nobel Prize.
Ten years since they began their quest,
 Not one of them had once digressed,
Each had been equal to the test,
By themselves devised.

And yet, they still had their detractors,
If we should heed such malefactors
We'd have no nuclear reactors,
A chilling thought.
Their carping would have kept us from,
Developing the atom bomb,
Napalm, nerve gas, I could go on,
Perhaps I ought.

You can bet we'd have never seen
Computers, videos, fax machines,
And what a godsend they have been,
You must admit,
And don't forget DNOC,
And Paraquat, and DDT,
Without them, just where would we be?
Don't think of it!

Yet this disruptive element,
Had their one day in parliament,
To spout their message of dissent,
Democracy!
But at the reading of the bill,
To sell the rich fruits of their skill,
The great British public had their will,
As you will see.

The Green member, a blonde, named Grey,
A pretty thing, wide eyed, and fey,
Said, "You'll be signing lives away,
Please, please, don't do it."
The Independent member's speech,
(A lay preacher, who'd come to preach)
Was, "If God's holy laws you breach,
You will live to rue it."

But the minister, witty and gay,
Said," Friends, its' been quite wet today
But now the wets have had their say,
Let's send them packing
Make no mistake, let us take this chance,
This is no time for dalliance,
We've almost struck a deal with France,
So let's get cracking!"

The vote was carried, five to one,
The MP's trooped out, in the sun,
Well satisfied with what they had done,
The British way!
The patents, granted to Cellation,
To sell genetic innovation,
Was hailed in print, throughout the nation,
As G.E Day.

Ten life-forms were in those patents,
Ten years in the development,
Ten billion pounds had been well spent,
We all agreed.
Amoeba, made from splicing four,
A creature never seen before,
Designed to fight a silent war,
Was the first seed.

Like secret agents, they were sent,
And billions of their lives were spent,
Consuming toxic effluent,
 From water courses,
Just for an encore, they would graze,
Throughout the dreaming summer days,
On poison algae, (Grim malaise)
Like tiny horses.

There was a snag, I must relate,
The things continued to mutate,
Till anything they saw, they ate,
A bitter pill!
Washed out, onto the ocean floor,
They bred, as they'd never bred before,
Ate plankton, till there was no more,
And all the krill.

Plankton? It's just a sort of scum,
And not much use to anyone.
The ocean is cleaner now it's gone,
So I'm quite pleased!
It follows, as day follows night,
Some other creatures lost the fight.
I read this, so it must be right,
They were diseased!

Those whales and things, that are no more,
Were dying slowly, long before,
Infecting all the fish, for sure,
Good job they're gone!
But now, our rivers are like wine,
You can swim in them anytime,
(Though some keen swimmers have gone blind)
Its lots of fun.

The second patent for Cellation,
Was an incredible creation,
And guaranteed to rid the nation,
Of rodent beasts,
A microscopic virus that,
Fused to a gene from a dead cat,
Was introduced into a rat,
Which was released.

And when the virus took a hold,
The rats became insanely bold,
And sallied outside, in the cold,
Looking to fight.
And any other rat they saw,
Immediately, they went to war.
Before too long, there were no more.
Eternal night!

Worldwide, unqualified success,
(Except for cleaning up the mess)
Cellation was a name to bless,
Their logo kissed.
Rattus, Rattus was extinct,
House mouse, fieldmouse, polecat mink,
Harvest mice were on the brink.
They won't be missed.

Another warrior took the field,
To fight, to kill, to never yield,
Not so the foe, its fate was sealed,
Death was its doom!
For it was aphids, green and white,
Who had forfeited the very right,
To live, and breathe, and see the light,
Of sun and moon.

A wonderful bacterium,
Makers aphid's skin tight as a drum,
And when it is warmed up by the sun,
It bursts apart.
Fanatics, all around the planet,
Said it was evil, we should ban it!
The rest of us told them to can it,
They soon lost heart!

Now aphids are a memory,
It hardly seems a loss to me,
To have our parks and gardens free,
Of insect pests,
I'm not the sort of fool who cries,
 For beetles, bugs, and butterflies,
 Felt no regret at their demise,
Its' for the best.

Cellation gave the world the Skenny,
One animal derived from many,
This wonder beast cost not one penny,
In special feeds.
Their appetites were just unreal,
Dead leaves, they thought a gourmet meal,
Newspaper, sawdust, orange peel,
Fulfilled their needs.

Tip out the refuse from the bin,
And eagerly, they'd take it in,
Broad in the back, with dark red skin,
Yellow beneath.
The beast is easy to deride,
Its' short, and round, and flat, and wide,
With more legs than a football side,
And rows of teeth.

But all at once there was a rash,
Of farmers, waving wads of cash,
To make good money, out of trash,
It was a dream!
The British minister's submission,
Made to the EEC commission,
For once, not treated with derision,
A worthy scheme,

Thanks to the pressure he exerted,
Farm subsidies were soon diverted,
And barns and stables were converted,
To skenny houses.
Some people said the scheme was rash,
The whole idea, a waste of cash,
Give them a plate of skenny hash,
And no' one grouses.

The trouble was, the little bores,
Were the world's first true omnivores,
When I say they could eat a horse,
Take it from me!
Two hundred, raging in the dark,
Once chewed their way out of their ark,
And through the orchard, stripped the bark,
From every tree.

The farmer's son was up at dawn,
Rubbing his eyes, he crossed the lawn,
To fetch a skenny, newly born,
For breakfast rashers,
The things they'd eaten, in the night,
Had sharpened up their appetites,
They scuttled through the brightening light,
With gleaming gnashers,

In terror then, he turned and ran,
They caught him by the farmer' van,
They say he was the only man,
 Whose breakfast ate him.
They ate his hat and boots as well,
Then headed for the house, pell -mell.
The farmer screamed "Oh bloody Hell,"
I quote verbatim.

A tidal wave poured through the door,
And through the farmhouse, four by four,
They ate the dog and cat before,
Father and mother,
They ate the coats from off the door,
They ate the carpet from the floor,
And then, when they could find no more,
They ate each other!

Infected by some devil's seed,
The madness spread throughout the breed,
And when, at last, it did recede,
They were all gone.
The farming world was devastated,
Farmers and stock were decimated,
"We have learned a lot," The PM stated,
"Life must go on."

"These are momentous risks we take,
Of course, we knew some eggs must break,
If we were ever going to make,
The omelette.
To all who said we all would lose,
I have some quite amazing news,
The exchequer, from its revenues,
Has paid the debt."

This wondrous news calmed all their fears,
The chamber rang with loud "Hear, hears,"
We'd paid off all those old arrears,
Thanks to Cellation.
And, in the following debate,
The Under Secretary of State,
Said, "Once more, Britain can be great,
A leading nation."

For it was said then, of Cellation,
A multi-national corporation,
That half the planet's population,
Was buying shares,
If someone, sometimes voiced a doubt,
Then he was quickly put to rout,
Big money carries lots of clout,
In men's affairs,

The ozone, on the edge of space,
Had more holes than a piece of lace,
Smear UV40 on your face,
Or you would fry.
The greenhouse gases hung up there,
And slowly heated up the air,
The loony fringe cried in despair,
"The end is nigh!"

Designer microbes, never fear,
Released into the stratosphere,
Had done the trick, within a year,
Of their deployment,
They gobbled up the CO_2,
And chlorofluorocarbons too,
Until the shrinking ice caps grew,
In sheer enjoyment.

Some scientists called into question,
The by-products of this ingestion,
Cellation's man, said, "Indigestion,
It should be known,
The biochemical reaction
In their alimentary tracts,
(I won't go into all the facts)
Makes pure ozone."

No more would dull and cloudy days,
Mar all our summer holidays,
Day after day, the sun would blaze,
Down on the beach,
And in those days, we saw, at last,
Those glorious summers of the past,
There was still one iconoclast,
Who loved to preach,

The independent, met before,
Still carried on his "Holy war"
Defending, "God and nature's law,
From mammon's greed."
The people laughed the fool to scorn,
One day they found him, stripped, and shorn,
Shattered, battered, bruised, and torn,
A broken reed.

By then, of course, I was not poor,
I was in there, on the ground floor,
And when Cellation's fortunes soar,
Then so do mine,
In England, I had built a home,
One in Geneva, one in Rome,
And friends, I did not live alone,
Nor did I pine,

For" Third world tribesmen," Useful phrase,
Who had perished from some weird malaise,
Out by our pool sides we would laze,
Champagne on ice.
And if you would like to go to war,
For primitives, then just be sure,
You have a good solicitor,
That's my Advice.

In recent years, lakes have run dry,
Great forests have begun to die,
No one quite knows the reason why,
A mystery!
Ecologists say its' a stage,
Climatic changes could presage,
The coming of the next ice age,
But don't ask me.

The genius of the great Cellation,
Financial mainstay of the nation,
Was brought to bear on procreation,
Or how to stop it.
Some species (It had been decreed)
Were little better than a weed,
Since they fulfilled no useful need,
They had to cop it.

One animal we all detest,
The rabbit, that perennial pest,
Was chosen to provide the test,
You would have smiled,
A group of the unwholesome beasts,
Were force-fed an unusual feast,
Of virus stew, then were released,
Into the wild.

In that first year, the virus spread,
The rabbit's young were all born dead,
"Bullseye," Cellation's spokesman said,
With boyish zeal.
Five bugs the boffins modified,
Transformed the English countryside,
The diplomat from Oz arrived,
To make a deal.

"Australia has the feral cat,
Which makes the bush its' habitat,
And there in numbers, has grown fat,
On local fauna.
And if you buggers get my gist,
Your bloody foxes just exist,
By eating what the cats have missed,"
He fought his corner.

"These are just two plagues, thanks to you,
Using our country as a zoo,
But we have Bloody rabbits too."
The man was peeved.
Cellation's man said, "Please don't shout,
If you have the financial clout,
We have the means to help you out,
Would you believe?"

"Australians took those creatures there,
It is Australia's cross to bear,
But one which we'll be glad to share."
It made me proud!
To see the nations stand in line,
To pick from that genetic vine,
Which was all British by design
A grateful crowd.

Those were the days of inspiration,
And marketing their own creations,
We saw the flags of every nation,
Proudly unfurled,
Genetic blueprints, bought and sold,
All nature mastered, we were told,
Our very futures were controlled,
A brave new world!

The world has changed since then, I fear,
I warned them it would end in tears,
Five babies in the last ten years,
Were born alive,
The schools are empty, echoing places,
The streets are full of ageing faces,
Humanity has come to stasis,
Can we survive?

Its' not my fault the world's grown cold,
I always said they were too bold,
That if scientists were uncontrolled,
They would enslave us,
The landscape is so stark and bare,
It's getting hard to breathe the air,
They've let us down. Its' just not fair.
Oh Jesus, save us!

Of course, this is just fantasy,
For we all know the powers that be,
Won't sanction such insanity,
So don't take fright,
Our politicians, good and wise,
Would never tell the people lies,
So little darlings, close your eyes,
God bless, good night.

When the wall came down.

"Oh, comrades all, can it be so?
Freedom at last, in this great land,
The finest hour we'll ever Know,
Can you believe? It is at hand,
Shoulder to shoulder we will stand,
We will take this freedom now in hand,
And never more will let it go!"

"Come, come to me, my little one,
I have such fear, see how I shake.
As soon as darkness comes, we'll run,
And take what little we can take,
The sleeping tiger is awake,
We must go, for your sweet life's sake,
The wind of change blows cold my son."

"For too long has the tyrant's yoke,
Held us bound to their dread treadmill,
Borne down upon the common folk,
Stunted our lives, stifled our will,
Stolen our heritage, until,
We said, "No more, we've had our fill."
Last night our glorious leader spoke.

Spoke of a nation's reborn pride,
And of a people long betrayed,
And from their ancient land denied,
Where now those vile sum-humans played,
Steeped in their filth, lived to degrade,
This land our proud forefathers made,
Where shall those foul usurpers hide?"

"No, leave grandfather here with me,
And you must take the little one,
For here our hearts will always be,
And we have grown too old to run.
The chances are they'll never come,
Remember, God protects his own.
Granddaughter, do this thing for me."

"God give us strength in this, our cause,
For this our heroes fought and died,
Let no man from beyond these shores,
Call our great struggle" Genocide."
For God and right are on our side,
God's will can never be denied,
War without mercy, let, or pause."

"Your dear Papa is gone I fear
Three days, since he went out for meat,
(My own true love, my heart, my dear)
Kalashnikovs out in the street,
I hear their heavy tramping feet,
Close in my arms, my little sweet.
Surely they'll never find us here?"

The man who hated trees.

I knew a man who feared and hated trees,
Just mention trees to him, his eyes would glaze,
He'd lived his life, besieged by enemies,
Who'd rustle down at him in baleful ways,
Wantonly toss their branches in the breeze,
Waving in weird and sinister displays,

He moved into our village, God knows why,
In eighty-four, the second week in May,
The tender leaves fresh green, against the sky,
Birds building nests, bright blossoms, lambs at play,
But Harry viewed it all with jaundiced eye,
"There'll be some changes here," I heard him say,

Before too long, his strategy was planned,
The lines of battle drawn, the air was tense,
A stand of poplars grew upon his land,
Rowans and silver birch against the fence,
He came out of his shed, chainsaw in hand,
For Harry had the means of his defence.

He said, "They're lousy trees, them poplars are,
There's no end to the damage they can do,
The wind can blow 'em over on your car,
If you stand under them, they'll fall on you,
Them are the worst of all the trees, by far,
Take my advice and cut all yours down too."

"You always see 'em growing outside churches,
I'd burn 'em down," He shuddered as he spoke,
And as for all them mountain ash, and birches,
My wood burner will send 'em up in smoke,
You'll see no birds in here, I'll have their perches,"
He laughed, delighted with his little joke.

He cycled home each evening from the station,
Legs pumping grimly through the homeward rush,
His eyes alight with fierce anticipation
Lined features glowing with a hectic flush,
To launch himself into the vegetation,
And rid his land of any kind of bush.

For Harry was a man who had a mission,
 His life devoted to his holy war,
Fighting an endless battle of attrition,
Appalled at all tall flora that he saw,
He would consign all green things to perdition,
That grew more than six inches from the floor.

He had an ancient bench, a single seater,
Each evening, he would sit there, at his ease,
And waited, with an old two-two repeater,
Which always lay across his bony knees,
To shoot at all the birds, he called "Seed eaters,"
And hated, only slightly less than trees.

The willow trees were dying in the valley,
Harry could see then from his upper floor,
Suspicion's finger pointed straight at Harry,
Though no one could be absolutely sure,
He was a favourite client of O'Malley,
The man who runs the local hardware store.

Each man has his own way that he relaxes,
Eases the tensions, wipes away the frowns,
Forgets his tribulations, debts, and taxes,
Life's unkind binds designed to drive you down,
Harry browsed through the poisons, saws, and axes,
In Pat O'Malley's hardware store in town.

He'd bought two packs of stump eradicator,
Every known brand of herb and pesticide,
All the mole, rat, and mouse exterminator,
His good friend Pat O'Malley could provide,
He took his leave of Pat, "I'll see you later,"
Picked up his purchases and went outside.

The sultry Autumn afternoon was long gone,
And Harry viewed the heavens without zest,
The lowering overcast obscured the pale sun,
Black thunderheads boiled over from the West,
And Harry, shambling homeward, at a half run,
Cursed Michael Fish, John Ketley, and the rest.

He steered clear of the big trees, on his way back
Heading across the golf course at a trot,
He wouldn't hear the fizzle, or the loud crack,
Would have no premonition of his lot,
A streak of lightning sizzled from the cloud wrack,
And barbequed poor Harry on the spot!

The reverend Jenkins wittered on with unction,
Of our good friend who'd given up the ghost.
Who'd shuffled off the coil. Who'd ceased to function,
Who'd run his race, and passed the winning post
Some vicars talk such tosh, without compunction,
And Jenkins is a bigger prat than most.

He said, "We must commemorate the life-force,
Of this fine man, who we all loved so well,
Perhaps a plaque, that all who pass it, might pause,
Learn from the simple tale that it will tell,
A stand of poplars grows, now, on the golf course,
And marks the very spot where Harry fell.

Chameleon.

She mooches through the house, a shapeless thing,
Slippers with turned-up toes, a sack-like robe,
Like Friar Tuck in drag, her hair a bush,
And a face on her to sour the milk.
The sun is bright, she doesn't want to know,
I make the tea. She leaves it to go cold,
She's down. I empathise, yet part of me,
Would dearly love to kick her through the door.

I'm in the bathroom, scraping at my face,
And now she's in the doorway, dressed to kill,
We go out to the shops, the day is fine,
Sleek as a cat, the woman, at my side,
Walks gaily through the town, a beauteous child,
Soft highlights in the dark sheen of her hair,
Lustrous eyes, soft pouting lips, a flashing smile,
I am entranced, I want to take her home.

A spectrum of worlds.

Last night once again, in my dreams,
I walked on the mountains of Mars,
And looked up, to the far-away gleam,
Through black emptiness, fearsome and cold,
To the planet which gave me my birth
.

Red dust, at my alien feet, swirls,
Drifts vapour-like briefly, and dies,
In thin air, once so rich on this world,
When violet clouds sailed amber skies,
Long before the first waking of earth.

Blue peaks, cloud-capped, misty with rain,
Pale green rivers etched the red land,
The wind sang across the great plain,
Bright water dimpled the sand,
And bright promise crackled the air

For life was astir in the deep,
And its story was on the first page,
While the far golden earth was asleep,
Yellow fire lighting her slumbering rage,
The red planet was young and was fair.

A vastness of time, come and gone,
A mere mote, in a physicist's eye,
The life of a world almost done,
When a massive rock bursts from the sky,
To the trembling hills. At the blow,

A great mountain of Mars is no more,
Than charred fragments, a thousand miles high,
The red ball vibrates to the roar
The shock rolls around the black sky,
And all is fell darkness below.

A meteor shower lights up the night,
 And the single-cell voyagers ride,
In chariots of fire, in their flight,
Through red clouds, to earth's saffron tide,
From their birthplace, a lifetime away.

Could those great asteroids be the bees,
Which can pollinate worlds as they die?
Those creatures from Mars, could it be,
You slept with one last night, so did I,
Weird, I know, even so, who can say?

There's a monster.

There's a monster in my bedroom,
Waiting for me every night,
I can hear his eerie silence,
After Mom turns out the light,
I lie there with eyes wide open
Watching shapes form in the room,
The begin to hear him moving,
Creaking, creeping round the room.

Are they footfalls in the darkness?
Was that an intake of breath?
Something seemed to touch my bedclothes,
I lie rigid, cold as death,
If I reach to turn the light on,
Will my hand touch skin, or hair?
Hide my hands beneath the blankets,
Dry eyes staring, What's out there?

Something drifting past the window,
Moving shadows round the wall!
What's that, standing by the wardrobe?
Was it really there at all?
I know it's just imagination,
When the morning sun is bright,
But there' a monster in my bedroom.
He'll be there again tonight!

Getting got.

My friends, this life can be a struggle,
You don't need me to tell you that,
There are more things to burst your bubble,
Than bristles, on the old doormat,
Where lie missives, in no way appealing,
In their livery of buff-ish hue,
From fellows short of fellow feeling,
Who want their pound of flesh from you.

You may see, "Please," You may see, "Thank you,"
Don't be misled, they're not your friends,
You can kid yourself, but to be frank, you,
Just know they'll get you in the end.
You can be sure, they're in no hurry,
The more they wait, the more you'll pay,
They are the lions, you the quarry,
The predators, and you the prey.

This analogy may be overstated,
You're not actually eaten by the pride,
But may well feel eviscerated,
And as badly chewed as if they'd tried,
You may feel that they get their kicks,
Of evil joy, to see your loss,
But no, they're wise to all your tricks,
But really, they don't give a toss

Unless you're of the chosen few,
For then, a penny in the pound you'll pay
Your good friend, Dave, smiles down at you,
The taxman looks the other way!

Weather report,

The day was wet, the day was cold,
One for umbrella's, scarves, and hats,
With prospect of more of the same,
I would not wish it on a rat!
But I was warm, and didn't care,
A good fire, blazing in the grate,
Though I knew I could not stay there,
I had to go out, soon or late.

So, out into the storm I went,
To do this thing that must be done,
Into the driving rain I bent,
Not what I'd categorize as fun,
Coming along, the other way,
A slight form, muffled to the eyes,
Though mummified, I have to say,
It was a shape I recognized.

From days when pretty dresses clung,
And long, tanned legs, that fascinated,
Picked their way through the doggie dung,
With which our paths are decorated,
Just as we passed, she fell, I caught her!
You've seen such stuff, in Mills and Boon,
I saved her from the poo-stained water,
But knew I must release her – soon.

But my luck was in, the day was charmed,
She had turned her ankle in the fall,
I lifted her in my strong arms,
Those gym fees paid off, after all!
She moaned, "Oh, oh," I held her close,
As in my fevered dreams. The thrills,
Went through me, like an overdose,
Of those small uplifting pills.

But I'm a gentleman, my face,
Betrayed no evil thoughts, I'm sure,
I carried her back to my place,
Hung her wet things on the door,
And set her down, before the fire,
Her injured ankle, on a heap,
Of cushions. I would be a liar,
If I denied my pulse's leap,

Though I'd known her, in a way, for years,
When I brought hot drinks and biscuits for us,
Her shy whispered "Thank you," To my ears,
Was like the Hallelujah Chorus.
I admit, the sweet girl at my fire,
Had she not been quite such a pet,
Less of an object of desire,
Could still be outside, getting wet.

But it was so good to sit and talk,
Sometimes, I think we just don't bother,
But luckily, she couldn't walk,
And so, we got to know each other,
I have to say, I love the way,
She walks today, my lovely wife,
Strange how a grey, and rainy day,
Brought warmth and sunshine to my life.

A moment in time.

During the "War to end all wars," An English infantryman
had a German soldier in his sights, and in easy range. The
Englishman did not shoot, but allowed the young German
to escape. The German soldier's name was Adolph Hitler.

He fell headlong, sprang up, and was away,
The ravaged earth erupting all around,
Ran madly, wildly, slipping in the clay,
To where a shell had opened- up the ground,
Crashed down on one, who had lain there awhile,
Half sunk in earth, yet grinned up, at the sky,
Arms spread, stained teeth bared, in a rictus smile,
"Life's hell my friend, better by far to die,"

Crouched, shaking, as the barrage died away,
He looked around, and knew he was alone,
His comrades blown to Hell, why not just stay,
Here with his new-found friend, of skin and bone,
Knees sunk in slime, his chin on clammy mud,
He pondered life and death, impartially,
Ahead, the shattered remnants of a wood,
And there, in easy range, the enemy.

Secure now, in the shell hole he had found,
He sighted, elbows cushioned in soft mud,
Calmly, across the awful, littered ground,
To where, in bright sunshine, the target stood.
But then, the crouching soldier thought to see,
In that slight form, in mud-stained field grey,
Rumpled and drab, another such as he,
Sick to the heart and wearied by the day.

The power that he held, was life and death,
To take a bitter vengeance, or to give,
Another precious day. With bated breath,
He let the muzzle fall, and whispered, "Live,"
The strange and silent figure raised his head,
Pale eyes scanning, across a sea of mud,
To where the soldier lay among the dead,
Then turning, disappeared, into the wood.

No peal of thunder, as he turned away,
No darkening sky, no tremor shook the ground,
A single moment, in the clamour of the day,
Silently come. And gone without a sound.
No bolt of lightning streaked down from the void,
The God of Abraham, slept on his throne,
The day the curse of Satan was deployed
To walk abroad, unknowing, and unknown,

Until the black worm, growing in his brain,
Stared from his shadowed eyes, and darkness fell,
Across the world, then people cried, in vain,
To heaven, out of the reeking depths of hell,
Was he unmoved, unmoving, at their loss?
The one, who for their sin's redemption, died,
While, steeped in Victim's blood, a broken cross,
Bore witness to a nation, crucified.

Superstition.

I'm not superstitious, though I don't walk under ladders,
Something could fall on me from above,
I've got a rabbit's foot, but that's just something I had, as,
A little gift from someone who I love,
I may sometimes cross my fingers when I do the lottery,
But honestly, that's just my bit of fun,
And lucky stars and horoscopes, don't mean a jot to me,
! read them, but then, so does everyone.

On Friday the thirteenth, I know I stayed home all day,
I just felt like a day of total ease,
It's easy to explain why my house number is 12A,
The hardware store had ones, but had no threes,
Now anyone would shudder when a black cat crossed his
way,
If you think, its only basic common sense,
Trip over him, your ankle goes, you lose a fortnight's pay,
Nothing to do with dread presentiments.

When I was a boy, I would avoid the pavement cracks,
A kid's game, just like hopscotch, or kick-ball,
Now I don't even bother, if you want to know the facts,
And the devil hasn't had me, after all!
I am not superstitious, when I broke the looking glass,
It was just with anger that I shook,
I'm not superstitious, I can still – oh, damn and blast,
I've said it three times now, that is bad luck!

In the Midst of Life.

"I love to hunt," the old man grinned, "To set my snare,
Baited with cunning, primed, and laid with care,
And then, at break of dawn, to find my prey,
Teeth bared, eyes bulging, in a frozen stare.
And I can tempt him to his fate with ease,
Knowing the nature of the little beast,
A mouldy cube of rancid mousetrap cheese,
Must seem to him, a most enticing feast,
You say he must have died, in agony,
In some dark musty corner of my house,
In truth, that couldn't matter less to me,
For, when all's said and done, he's just a mouse."

I would have said the same, when I was young,
And used to know the old head-keeper, John,
Who, in those days, managed the estate,
Where my dad worked. We had a lot of fun,
He always used to call me, "Little mate,"
And he would often let me tag along,
He knew every wild thing that roamed the woods
Though none of them, it seemed, were friend to John.
More than once, I heard him say, that if he could,
"He'd kill the buggers, every single one."
Except the game, o' course," I understood,
They were reserved for killing later on.

At dawn, when we would walk the woodland ways,
He would show me where those lifeless beasts still lay,
With rigid, gaping jaws, and glassy eyes,
Transfixed in the iron traps which they had sprung,
Some lay, half throttled, staring, still alive,
John would dispatch them then, with boot, or gun,
Sometimes his master, on his morning ride,
Called down in passing, "You've been busy, John,"
And John's broad russet face would flush with pride,
Death always pleased his lord, which pleased old John.

And the white hunter, under Kenya's trees,
Lives by the very same philosophies,
The men with credit cards, demand the best,
And everyone, it seems, must aim to please,
He takes his eager client, and they go,
To where, some days ago, he built a hide,
And there, they watch a huge black buffalo,
Browsing, along the quiet waterside
"Oh, he's a beauty, sir, don't miss this chance,
You're never going to find much better game,
Just rest your rifle barrel on this branch,
I think you'll find it helps you with your aim."

They watch the great beast turn his head, and freeze,
At an odd sound, in the whisper of the trees,
Then stagger, as the high-powered rifle roars,
And bellowing, sink slowly to his knees,
Shuddering, pitching to the sodden ground,
To kick and flounder in the clinging mud,
And ooze, a final spasm, and all around,
An ever-widening pool of glistening blood.
Sounds of excited laughter, as he falls,
"Oh, wonderful shot, sir, one of your best,
That head will look impressive, on your wall,
The scavengers will take care of the rest."

Cheeks flushed, eyes shining with a modest pride,
The brave man, standing in that jungle hide,
Has travelled over half the world, to see,
Such majestic beasts as this, and shed their blood,
From that great homeland of the brave and free,
Where long ago, his own forefathers stood,
Fired with their visions of prosperity,
And golden dreams, of a new nationhood,
They saw, "From shining sea, to shining sea,"
A mighty land, and saw that it was good,
"All this belongs," They said, "To you and me,
Made for us, by the very hand of God."

But their bright vision had a fatal flaw,
Even dreamers such as they, could not ignore,
God's wondrous gift, was only second-hand,
For others, who had been there, long before,
Knowing that their own gods gave them the land,
Stood in the way, and simply had to go,
Their lands annexed, their many tribes dispersed,
And rotting mountains of dead buffalo,
Bore silent testimony to the force,
Of ideals, and golden dreams, metamorphosed,
To the dire, and bloody dreams of carnivores,
Calling on, " Father, son, and holy ghost."

Let me in.

So many people I have known,
Could smile, that brave, long-suffering smile,
All through a life, painful, and hard,
The bitterest of fates, may hurl,
Its slings and arrows, still they smile,
Heaven will be their just reward

They know, you see, the good they do,
In their brief sojourn on this earth,
Will be repaid, a millionfold,
For them, sweet paradise awaits,
And endless blessings they will know,
When at last, they rest within the fold,

Of The Good Shepherd, for they know,
Their God chastises those He loves,
They can rejoice in life's abuse,
Endure, through poverty, and pain,
Never bemoan the direst fate,
For them, their agony is proof

Of joys to come, beyond the veil.
How I envy them their certainty,
Wish I could feel the way they feel,
To take life's buffets with a smile,
To join them, in their fantasies,
The happiness they know, is real.

Zoo and Pig on the Town.

They ate chips from their polystyrene nests,
Dropping the used containers on the ground,
Outside the youth club, by the litter bin,
Zoo stamped on both of them, he liked the sound,
Took out the trusty marker from his jeans,
And wrote a comment on the youth club wall
"You're all wierdos in this place," He'd never been,
Inside, "And never would mate," After all.
He'd seen the sort of dorks who use the place,"

Pig laughed, "Yeh mate, I've seen em, oh 'kin 'ell,
Have you seen them poncey tops they wear,
With, "We're in the club," on 'em, you can tell,
Wild horses wouldn't drag my arse in there."
They strolled across the leisure centre car park,
Kicking a plastic bottle as they went,
Pig keyed a gleaming Lexus, made his mark,
While Zoo, kicking at the door, gave vent,
"Yeh, that'll wipe the smug look off His face."

They swaggered, laughing, past the bowling alley,
The theatre, boxing club, and snooker hall,
Where Zoo and his marker added to the tally,
Scrawling a giant penis on the wall,
Next to a poster, "Soccer, come and train,
All welcome, if you think that you can play."
Said Zoo, "Yeh, catch me, out there in the rain,
Chasin' a football, that'll be the day,

C'mon, let's go and use our public loo."
After using the phone booth, (As they always did,)
Pig flashed his last two fags, dropping the packet,
Saying, "This place didn't seem too bad, as kids,
But lately, well, I'm not sure I can hack it,"
Zoo wrenched a "Keep Left" bollard from its moorings,
And swore, Pig said, "What's got into you?"
"It's this 'kin town," Said Zoo, "Man, it's so boring,
It grinds you down, there's just sod all to do,"

Opacity,

This wall,
we've built,
around us,
yes, I think,
Its working
pretty well,
they can't
See
In.

There is
a downside
though, I have
My doubts.
While they're
Not seeing in
We can't
See
Out.

The forest hunter.

On a farm I knew as a child, half-wild cats lived and bred
They kept the rats down, and so were tolerated,
until the farmer judged that they had become too
numerous, or maybe just felt like killing something.
Then he would come out.
With his twelve- bore.

He never had a name, the forest hunter,
Born half-wild, to a mangy farmyard moggie,
And playing in the sunshine, with his brothers,
He saw the farmer at the gate, just watching,
The five black siblings with their mother, rolling,
Play-fighting, in the sun-warm rickyard,
Saw the flash of white teeth, the red face, grinning,
And saw something, long, and black, and shining,

A sudden awful roar, and then the others,
In bloody shreds, and somehow, he was running,
Stumbling blindly over straw- strewn cobbles,
Crying now, out through the wind-blown barley,
To the wildwood then, where darkness found him,
Still trembling, high up in a mighty oak tree,
Just as far from earth, and from the horror,
As his tiny, scrambling claws could take him.

Clinging all that night, among the branches,
The fear that held him fast, gave way to hunger,
He fed, at first, on insects, grubs, and beetles,
But before the first day's end, his hunger drove him,
Back down the tree, into the old leaf litter,
And there, the instincts of his race took over,
For soon he found the timid creatures, creeping,
Round the oak tree bole, were easy pickings.

The start and end of night, a time of plenty,
At dusk, he killed, and when the dawn was breaking,
And with the rising of the sun, was sleeping,
In a squirrel nest, well hidden in the foliage,
Fearing the farmer, and his kind by daylight.
Time passing, in the dray he slept, and grew,
Grew in strength, and grew, as well, in cunning,
Dread nemesis now, of those he hunted.

A thing of darkness waits, of tooth and claw,
As twilight fades, creatures of night are stirring,
Leaving warm nests to forage, hot hearts beating,
And staring eyes, a single breath away,
From life's end, and that final shriek, despairing,
As the black assassin leaps from shadows,
With vicious fangs to pierce, with claws to rend,
Taking their living flesh into his own.

Two boys, two catapults, an Autumn day,
Another summer gone, the bright leaves turning,
They fire their pebbles up into the dray,
A scream of rage or pain, a moving shape,
Flies, hissing, down the oak, a half- seen blur,
Between them, disappearing through the ferns,
Leaving an image seared into their minds,
Glossy black fur, green eyes, red mouth agape,
Spitting its hate. The boys stand eye to eye,

Rigid, hair on end, chilled to the bone.
When they tell their tales, the boys are greeted,
With smiles of scorn, and grins of disbelief,
But then, the tale is just too good to founder,
Instead, somehow has grown with every telling,
And soon, a massive red eyed cat is born,
There is a panther, in the wildwood, prowling,
All, it seems, have heard its fearsome howling.

And mothers tell their sons, "Keep from the woods,"
Some men take shotguns, searching for the beast,
The big cat, though, has left the oak, and moved,
Ever deeper now, into the pathless forest,
Found an old, ruined, charcoal burner's hovel,
The door ajar, dry leaves blown and fallen,
Over the years, the warmest bed he's known,
Since the haystack nest, where he was born.

Time passes, another winter come and gone,
Spring, and long days, sleeping in the sun,
The cat had reached the zenith of his powers,
Safe, in the secret place, deep in the wildwood,
The farmer fading slowly from his mind.
Some nights, a need, far stronger than his fear,
Would draw him, once again, back to the farm,
Where rats roamed in the dark, and he would kill,

Then, hunger stayed a while, would climb the bay,
Lie deep in hay, where the old dam bore him,
Where he had suckled, with his naked brothers,
Drawing with them, the warm milk, from his mother,
Before break of dawn, he would be moving,
Silently through the trees, back to his home-place,
Sometimes, the call of home eclipsed all hunger,
Sometimes he would kill, for killing's sake.

Eat a portion of his victim, and move onward,
Back to his hidden lair, roof deep in brambles.
To sleep again, secure, and far from men,
Spraying as he went, leaving his message,
For other toms to find, to heed his warning,
"I am male, I am strong. All this is mine!"
For years then, as the hunter roamed the forest,
Men talked of him, some of their tales were true.

A follower of the hunt, told of the day,
The hunt was out, a hound, strayed from the pack,
Had trapped the wild cat, cornered, in the brambles,
And lived its life from then, scarred, and half blinded.
The whipper-in, who saw the black shape, ghosting,
Out through thorn and bracken, disappearing,
Swore the thing had been more than a monster,
Black as the night, faster than any foxhound.
His legend grew, "The beast," became immortal.

All cats love night, whole cats are wild at heart,
Every tom is drawn, when queens are calling,
And every-one will fight, heeding that call,
But none could ever stand against the hunter,
He'd send them limping homeward, torn and bleeding,
Back to warm hearthrugs, tender loving care,
And battles won, covered the willing queen,
Sent his genes through generations yet unborn.
And disappeared again, back to the forest.

To kill, to eat, sleep warm, to be alone,
His nature was fulfilled, he was content,
But then a poacher, pushing through the tangle,
Stumbled, by chance, upon the ruined hovel,
Kicked at the broken door, and in the gloom,
Struck out at some black thing, green eyes shining,
Dropped his stick, cried out, and turned to run,
The hunter, screaming, clawed at him, in passing.
"No lie," He said, "I thought my time had come."
When he told his story later, in the bar.

But once again, the hunter had been found,
Moved on again, at last, he found a place,
To hide, inside a lightning-blasted willow,
And there he stayed, until the world was white,
Curled in a ball he lay, his strength was failing,
Brutal ice fingers probed him in the darkness,
A virus, multiplying, in his blood,
Drove him back to the farmyard; in the hay,
Snug now, in the soft hollow he had made,
He felt the welcome warmth seep to his bones.

Dreaming of summer days, of times long gone,
He slept, well past the rising of the sun,
And crossed the icy cobbles, half aware,
His vision blurred, a buzzing in his head,
The virus in his bloodstream, was a storm,
And ancient scars, from battles he had fought,
Seemed fresh again, each one a shard of pain,
The farmer's shotgun, blew the cat apart,
Into the snow, the light gone from his eyes,
He went from life to death, without a thought!

Unlucky numbers.

The prick of thorns, the sting of bees,
Some say that bad luck comes in threes,
The dog that bites, the cat who scratches,
Others may say, it comes in batches.

To bark your shin on something rough,
You may say once would be enough,
To hit your thumbnail with a hammer,
Not a time for numbers, more for grammar.

Two lucky dice, and a rabbit's foot,
Won't boost your chances, when you put,
Your hard-earned cash, at ten to one,
On a horse, who's forgotten how to run,

With three legs working, as legs should,
And another one that's made of wood,
A jockey, too, who, on the quiet,
Has just got fed up with his diet.

A friend of mine, stood by the road,
When a cement lorry shed its load,
Bad luck with knobs on, for my mate,
Delivered by the hundredweight.

Another chap (He's still extant)
Was squashed flat, by an elephant,
There, under Kenya's blazing sun,
He got his bad luck by the ton.

The fiftieth time, that you get lumbered,
You may think old Nick has your number,
For sixty-five days last year, it's true,
Fate may have dropped you in the poo,

Don't moan and groan, sing paeans of praise,
You had three hundred lucky days.

Get a grip,

My image scowled out from the looking glass,
In my tight distressed jeans, and leather bomber,
Sparse strands of hair stretched thin, across my head,
Not unlike a flat back four, with two sent off,
Run ragged, trying hard, to do their job,
And of those who hadn't hung around for long.

Had to admit, I really looked an ass,
In the trendy, "Ray Ban" shades I bought last summer,
The polo shirt, in fifty shades of red,
To wake up to yourself, it can be tough,
I spoke aloud, "Let's face the facts, you slob,
You're an old fool, still pretending to be young."

Later that morning, in the barber's chair,
"Take the lot off! Give me a number one."
And soon, my precious hair was on the floor,
"Good Lord," I said, "I've had a rush of blood,"
"No sweat mate, sure, your Barnet's on the mat,
A month from now, you'll be tying it in a braid."

"Don't worry about it, pal, its only hair,
Right now, you may be thinking it's all gone,
Before you know it, you'll have grown some more,
Lucky for me. But no joke, Mate, it looks good,
Much better than it was." He would say that,
Of course, after all, it is his trade,

A bunch of Oxfam bags, under my arm,
Man on a mission, I headed up the stairs,
Went through my drawers and wardrobes, in a rage
When I ran my hand over my number one,
The image in the glass, gave me a grin,
An old fool, who had come to terms with age.

Waiting.

Shivering, we stand together, in the street,
In icy drizzle, slanting down the drab,
Grey alleyways, just waiting for the day,
To come again, and warm these dismal stones,
The bitter night has chilled me to the bone.
Faith is a simple dream, yet still we pray,
Each to his private god, cold as the slab,
Or the oily water round our clammy feet.

It's all gone wrong again. My life is cursed,
I had a doorway, snug, out of the rain,
Let my mate, Zen, come in, he's not so bad,
We shared a soggy hamburger, a bag,
Of chips, a spindly roll-up, drag for drag,
He's gone soft in the head, a little mad,
And last night, we had a kicking for our pains,
From the evil bastard, who had got there first.

Zen sings, "God save the queen," Beneath his breath,
And seems to get some comfort from the song,
But she could build two shelters for the poor,
A month, nor feel the loss, though so hard earned,
From interest, her massive wealth returned,
Or miss a single pot of caviar,
To hear, "God save the Queen," Somehow seems wrong,
From skeletons in rags, waiting for death.

The truth will out.

We'd been in Benidorm three days, no longer,
The wife and me, sat in a beach-front bar,
Up roared this Spanish waiter, on his Honda,
Handsome, dark eyed, and slim (They always are)
As he came in, he looked straight at the missus,
Or so I thought, I know she looked at him!
These Latino guys, their looks are more like kisses,
I know I'd had a few, but I'm not dim.

The drink took over then, that's my excuse,
It often happens when I'm on the sauce,
Your inhibitions, and your tongue, get loose
I offered lover boy outside, of course,
He shook his head, she said, "Don't be a fool.
He'd flatten you." That just made me more vexed.
For three days now, he'd been there, at the pool,
Strutting about the place, flexing his pecs.

Like some Greek god, in flimsy budgie smugglers,
Me feigning sleep, but I was wide awake,
Comparing him to all us other strugglers,
She's sneaking looks, behind her "Take a Break."
Maybe it was all those breakfasts, snacks, and lunches,
I'd had, I did not land a single lick,
He must have got in fifteen lucky punches,
And followed them up with a lucky kick.

The bugger danced around me, in the fight,
As to some mad internal Latin rhythm,
Duffed badly up! I at least got one thing right,
When he roared off, my fecking wife went with him,
Absence, you know, does not make hearts grow fonder,
Through bleary eyes, I'd watched them ride away,
Her fat, shapeless rear, perched on that Honda,
Stays with me like a bad dream, to this day.

One thing I've learned,
Adversity makes you stronger,
I've lost three stone,
I'm slim,
I'm fit,
I'm gay.

Poverty's perks.

Good news my friends, at last I'm free,
No grim tax man hangs over me,
To batter a poor man to his knees,
Like a fleshly sword of Damocles,

No money lenders wait, out there,
To scrape my meagre barrel bare,
With outrageous interest on a loan,
From men who'd get blood from a stone,

No mortgage payments wring me dry,
No bills to make a brave man cry,
No heating charges chill my blood,
Tax up on drinks and fags? Well good!

I don't use either now, you see,
Or gas, or electricity,
I'm free of all that stuff. A pox,
On them, I've got a cardboard box!

Bad, but good.

It was early in the morning when I first saw darling Eva,
She was standing at the bus stop, on the corner of the street,
Small and slim, cute as a kitten, I was late, but could not leave her,
Her big brown eyes were soft and warm, her smile was sugar sweet,

In my mind, a plan was forming, as we said our first hello,
I called in, on my mobile, and the lies rolled off my tongue,
Somehow, I'd caught a fever (Well, at least that bit was so)
"I was sick, I had man flu," Well yes, I do know it was wrong,

"Where are you bound for, Eva? Are you really? Well, I never.
That's where I'm going too." I said, "I Hope we get some sun,"
"Oh, here's the bus now," she said, "Shall we sit together?
We can keep each other company if you like, it should be fun."

I was half a block from work, when we clambered on the bus,
For a guilty trip to pretty places, we had never seen,
By the time we said goodbye that day, me had turned to us,
And a drab, and dreary Monday morning turned into a dream,

And you know, that stolen day was all it took, to prove to me,
Though we're told, "Strive to be honest, true, and fair,"
When truth and honesty won't take you where you want to be,
Being sneaky, telling lies, will get you there.

Monuments to wasted lives.

On the bank from Canongate, up to the Roman Way,
In a neat estate of houses, tidy paths and lawns,
Pretty baby clothes are blowing on bright washing lines,
In air as clean, I suppose, as you'll find anywhere.
No sign remains, of what stood there, for many a day,
Before the proud young mortgagor's forebears were
born,
And stands there still, in the vague dreams of older
minds,
For whom that musty foundry smell still taints the air.

Which clung to every particle of metal dust,
Lying, like dirty blankets over everything,
That smell alone, could tell you, though you may be blind,
Of incandescent iron, and pattern-maker's sand,
Back from your week in Morecambe Bay, in mid- August,
Or your Easter trip to Dudley Zoo, in early Spring,
Clearer than words, that smell could speak into your
mind,
"Back to the grindstone, Jockey, you're a factory hand."

And the foundry buildings greeted you, when you arrived,
Their doleful shades of drabness, in the brightest sun,
Sucked light into the dusty walls, and gave back grey,
Crouching, like sombre monoliths, their gaping doors,
Would swallow you at seven, vomit you forth at five,
Into the bright Spring afternoon sun, almost gone,
And you hung your satchel on your bike, and rode away,
Free, until the morning rolled around once more.

At the grindstones stands a woman, young, and very fair,
Her buxom curves encased in a blue overall,
Rounded hips, in a sack apron, press the hard, grey,
Casting to the grindstone wheel, hot metal flies,
And scream and clamour echoes in the dusty air,
As she turns again, and lets the heavy casting fall,
Picking up the next of many, with a practiced sway,
And metal shards are rusting in her hazel eyes.

She turns to where a manly figure stands, close curling
hair,
Clings damply to that noble head, could he have been,
Leader of a Roman cohort, in another time,
 Or exchanging deep philosophies with Socrates,
But her lover is a foundryman, the white- hot glare,
Of molten iron, not sun, has lent his face its sheen,
And ruddy glow, the images that fill his mind,
Are of foaming pints, sex, football pools, and days of
ease,

Too few and far between, those bright red- letter days,
Too soon gone, consigned too soon to memory,
Watching Freddie Mills beat Lesnevich in Fifteen rounds,
Billy Wright, holding the cup aloft, at Wembley Stadium,
Being there, when Randy Turpin hammered Sugar Ray,
And last weekend, under the spreading Cockshutt trees,
When soft lips, and gentle arms, had turned his mind
around,
To think of her, and all the weekends, yet to come.

But now, once slender fingers, are arthritic claws,
Tight, blue-rinsed perm, lined features, and a painful walk,
Watching "East Enders," In her bungalow, with vacant mind,
She sips, absently, at a cooling cup of Nescafe,
But in dreams, she's often lifted in his arms once more,
Laughing children ride his shoulders, on a Sunday walk,
Across the Nabb, (Though tomorrow was back to the grind,
For five days and a half) Those were the shining days,

Which will stay, forever crystal clear in memory,
The children laughing in the sun, are far away,
Halfway across the world, with children of their own,
They had seen their ageing father, fighting hard for air,
After years of mindless toil, of dust and drudgery,
The rust-stains in their mother's eyes, and would not stay,
To bear the dreary burdens, she will live alone,
And die alone, and never say "This was not fair."

As a Parrot.

What is this love thing? It's a virus,
I caught mine from you, I think,
Breathing the same air you're breathing,'
That, or drinking from your drink,

Little motes, too small to measure,
Issued from your parted lips,
Felt strange, was it pain, or pleasure?
Then, next day, I get the grips,

Hot and cold by turns, all shaky,
Writing silly things on walls,
Stomach tied in knots, all evening,
Just because you didn't call,

Funny thing is, when I see you,
Get my dose of medicine,
Far from making me feel better,
More of the bugs find their way in.

It's your fault of course, I blame you,
If you had turned your face away,
I might not have breathed your virus,
And I would be okay today,

Come round, if you get this letter,
Come round please, and be my nurse,
Don't want you to nurse me better,
Baby, come and nurse me worse.

Leasehold.

Love, it's a sort of ownership, would you agree?
Perhaps "Leasehold," Is the best way to describe the deal,
You gave me a lease on you, it was not free,
I paid for it, by leasing part of me to you,
Not all, you'll notice, that would be a different thing,
That would be freehold you see, not limited by time,
And would indicate full ownership of property,
No chance, I fear, in contracts of the heart and mind.

For everyone holds something back, in every heart,
The deeds, if they were written, would be codified,
"The buyer shall not have deed of all, only a part,
And by the seller, access shall be circumscribed,"
It's a bit like leasing rooms in some big house,
Off course, there's access to your gaff, and rights of way,
But if you trespass outside agreed boundaries,
You'll get a warning letter friend, sure as the day.

You may be free to use the television room,
Or sit on the garden bench, (Not on the grass)
Little extras such as these, your landlord may allow,
Take liberties beyond them pal, and it's your ass,
Such is the case, with those contracts of, "Me and you,"
You lease just the percentage of the one you love,
That they are willing to allow you access to,
 Up to a predetermined line, and not above,

The system works quite well, okay, it's not ideal,
But what can you expect, this is the real world,
It's a pity that we tend to wear rose coloured specs,
Think we own more than we do. Not to be churlish,
I thought I owned the lease on you, I'd paid your price,
With a good bit more of me, I will tell you that!
I have always given more than taken, and it was not nice,
When your eviction notice landed on my mat!

The Ant.

I watched a tiny ant, on my backyard,
Tearing frenetically along, the way they do,
This way and that, over the slabs of stone.
What could justify such frantic haste?
But then, oh then, imagine the delight!
He had found a small, winged creature, in a crack,
Hoisted the dead thing, up onto his back,
And headed for the colony with joy.
How he would be feted, by the rest,
When he hauled his wondrous trophy to the nest.

I watched, as he plunged onward, with his load,
Madly, along the scent-trails leading home,
With undiminished haste, he zig-zagged over stones,
Despite the burden. Then, a sudden pause,
He had reached a place, where forage-trails had crossed,
And was nonplussed, then on again he ran,
All urgency, his little legs a blur,
"Come on my son," But then, another pause,
And off again he went, with desperate haste.

I watched with bated breath, willing him on,
Until he came back, to the very spot,
Where, long ago, it seemed, he'd found his prize,
And there, a tiny twig, across his path,
Sent the dead thing tumbling from his back,
And heedless of his loss, he scurried on,
Leaving his hard-won burden far behind,
In a crevice, for some other ant to find,

Take the plaudits he had so nearly won,
While he raced madly on, an also-ran.

The Nail.

The nail was driven, long ago,
 Into the cottage wall,
I heard it ring to every blow,
I saw the bright sparks fall.
How strange, the tricks the mind can play,
I see that day as yesterday,
And how that sunlit garden lay,
The blue sky over all

The arm that swung the hammer then,
Was sinewy and long,
This man, born of a time when men,
Of all things, must be strong,
To do their duty, not complain
Bend willing backs to take the strain,
Be stoic, in the face of pain.
Just such a man was John.

There was a time, between the wars,
It seems unreal now,
Boys, taking fallen father's chores,
Became as men, somehow,
A mother, who was no man's bride,
Born of a love, unsanctified,
Young Johnny was his mother's pride,
And joy, mine too, I vow.

Though Johnny was just seventeen,
He was a man to me,
We swore then, we would share our dream,
For all eternity,
Our love was sacred from the start,
For those, who God joins, heart to heart,
No mortal man should ever part,
But it was not to be,

Said John, "My lass, thy love is gold,
And more than gold, to me,
For gold is only bought and sold,
Thy love was given free,
I swear on this our wedding day,
As long as yonder oak shall stay,
Until that old nail rusts away,
I shall be true to thee."

Too soon, my Johnny had to go,
Where his father went before,
With passing years, I came to know,
I would see my love no more,
But the garden, through the season's run,
Shone, like a bright hope, in the sun,
As did the sign which hung there from,
The nail, above the door.

Just last week, came a violent storm,
It blew the great oak down,
It battered down, the fields of corn,
And strewed my flowers around,
At last, the old nail's time was done,
For now, the long years have rolled on,
When morning came, the nail was gone,
And the sign was on the ground.

A new nail was driven, yesterday,
Into the cottage wall,
The face is lined, the hair is grey,
My John still stands as tall,
As on that bright, remembered day,
If God is kind, here we will stay,
Where Shropshire's green hills roll away
The blue sky over all.

Love and Insomnia.

How warm, how very dark it is, my love,
In here, these friendly shadows are so deep,
I must picture your sleeping face, beside me,
As in many a waking dream,
When tender thought of you and I would move me,
Like a hunger-ache, bereft of sleep.
Cursing the bitter fates that would deride,
My wild delusions, and my foolish schemes.

They call this feeling love! Pathetic word,
For the sweet torment, I so keenly sought,
A gluttony, an all-consuming greed.
To take, and own another, I recall,
Watching you dance with someone once, and heard,
Your laughter, saw your upturned face, and thought,
How nice, to punch his face, to see him bleed,
All over that Armani suit, and fall.

Hate would have been the word then, or despair,
Standing with all the losers, at the bar,
Watching you dance, I just could not pretend,
To be a member of that sorry crew,
As you moved on the floor, a perfect pair,
Ideally matched, as couples seldom are,
I heard the foolish banter of my friends,
Wished him in Hell! And wished myself with you.

To hold you, as he did, a fantasy,
And yet tonight again, in this small room,
Mine are the arms around you, while you sleep,
And with the first grey light of the new day,
Your bright, disordered hair, soft arms tossed free,
Will wet the eyes that watch you, in the gloom,
Fool that I am! If only I could keep these moments,
But I feel them slip away,

As you will, I have seen it in your eyes,
A shadow of regret, a taking back,
Of something I thought given. Only lent,
In fact, that inch by inch, will be withdrawn,
Until at last, there's nothing but goodbye.
How many nights have I been on this rack?
How many sleepless hours have I spent?
Loving the dark, hating the coming dawn.

Boys, dogs and rabbits.

Little boys, and dogs, and rabbits,
In my time, I have known a few,
With the most revolting habits,
It's quite amazing what they'll do.
A rabbit, having eaten grass,
Will eat the same grass, once again,
And he saves himself the hassle,
Of chewing grass, out in the rain,

You may well think I'm being funny,
But it is quite true, take it from me,
That resourceful little bunny,
Is a currant factory,
You can tell he loves his food,
Its gourmet grub to him, that's plain,
As soon as Bunny can extrude it,
Bunny wolfs it down again.

The weirdest things are fascinating,
To a small boy, heaven knows,
He'll spend hours, investigating,
The interior of his nose.
If two boys get together, you can,
Bet standards are just bound to fall,
Pretty soon they're finding who can,
Wee the furthest up the wall.

Evolution strives, in stages,
For perfection, in the end,
Dogs have evolved, through countless ages,
Quite unique ways of making friends,
Out on the prowl, your average hound,
Communication on his mind,
Leaves messages, and gifts around,
For all the other dogs to find

When two dogs meet, with tails up curled,
They are very soon close friends, it seems,
For in that complex canine world,
The ends must justify the means,
In June, your dog finds the cadaver,
Of something, dead since January,
Rover will get into a lather,
Rolling around in ecstasy,

When bathed, and brushed, he's so appealing,
So cute and cuddly, you may think,
Old Rover does not share your feeling,
The dog would much prefer to stink.
Boys, dogs, and rabbits, though quite nice,
In many ways, a sheer delight,
Don't look too closely, that's my advice,
It just may spoil your appetite,

Shadows.

It was in that place of artificial horizons,
Where the unreal is, virtually, more than reality,
That macho, wild, rebellious young fellow,
Was never quite that young, and was a nice boy,
But was not what he seemed, though what he seemed,
Seemed more seemly, than in fact it was.

He saw himself, perhaps, as others saw him,
An icon of the young, rejector of old values,
Shining with a messianic light,
Leading his disciple into darkness,
He was not the first, though he seemed so,
Death, it seems, is the catalyst,

Converting the meagre to greatness,
And the great, to a sort of sainthood,
Conferring an endless half-life,
On the mangled victim,
Living out his phantom destiny,
In the vague minds,
Of believers,

Like an entity,
Shattered into shards,
The many parts,
Far greater,
Than was,
The sum.

In the Night.

The storm clouds had blown over, but the wind that
night,
Still blustered at the walls, and shadowy trees were
things,
Like unquiet spirits, bending in some pagan rite,
To mop and mow, in semblance of cold sentient beings,
Nodding, in seeming menace, from their world of grey,
Moving, as though to peer into his darkened room,
Then all the certainties of life were of the day,
While out there, ancient forces waited, in the gloom.

Midnight had come and gone, still in the dark, alone,
Rigid he lay, some sound had chilled him to the core,
The wind-sigh in the chimney, or a muffled groan?
Was he awake or dreaming? He could not be sure,
Something was in the house with him! Out in the hall,
A furtive creak, the stealthy closing of a door,
Outside his room, the faintest sound. A soft footfall?
Ears at the stretch, he lay. What was he listening for?

Outside, drab souls, dread entities, were back from Hell,
Again, to crawl, and hop, and slither up to see,
To grin with jagged teeth, into his fragile cell,
Staring in, at his cringing form, from every tree,
With knowing eyes, they leered at him, he felt their need,
An knew that very soon, his shaking walls would fall,
Then, heedless of his silent screams, they all would feed,
But shuddering, he awoke. A bad dream, after all.

Born of his fears, a self-created fantasy,
No horrors waited for him in the sombre night,
Yet the clammy hand of fear still would not set him free,
He reached the switch, to flood his little room with light,
His own pale image stared out, from the looking glass,
As he looked around the room, at his familiar things,
Reflected his wide eyes, mirrored his shaky laugh,
The paperbacks by Herbert, and the Stephen Kings

In rows upon the bookshelf, with a rueful smile,
He doused the light, and felt his way across the floor,
To sleep now, too exhausted by his dreams gone wild,
To ever hear the whisper of the opening door,
Or see their crouching shapes, drifting into the room,
Mouths gaped in silent mirth, reptilian eyes glowed red,
Teeth gleaming in the darkness, they began to croon,
As with long, scaly arms, they dragged him from his bed.

A poem for Kay.

Sometimes, when the rain is falling,
And the winter wind is chill,
Wouldn't it be quite enthralling?
If, just by an act of will,
You could make the clouds roll over,
And the bitter wind abate,
Filling all the fields with clover,
Honeysuckle round the gate.

Golden sunshine on the pasture,
Dreaming through the summer hours,
Butterflies, in silent rapture,
Fluttering through the scented flowers,
Song- birds, drowsing in the hedges,
To content to even sing,
Moorhen, creeping through the sedges,
Partridge, sleeping in the ling.

Summer is lovely in the city,
Flowered dresses everywhere,
But I know a place, so pretty,
Green and silent, and so rare,
You can hear the distant whirring,
Of the swallow's wings in flight,
Watch the beech leaves, gently stirring,
Filtering in, the dappled light.

Then, I feel such fierce elation,
In this secret place I've found,
If I could have such isolation,
I would never want to see a town.
People have to work, and worry,
People have to scrimp, and strive,
Can't be late! You'll have to hurry,
Nose to grindstone, nine to five.

Always plotting, always scheming,
Both eyes fixed upon the goal,
Trouble is, that while you're dreaming,
Like a goldfish, in a bowl,
Through the trees, the sun is streaming,
On a quiet, grassy knoll,
Out there, where the world is gleaming,
There, you could restore your soul.

Beasts of the Field.

Giraffe,
Balletic, and graceful,
Moving through the mists of dawn,
To forage, with your purple tongue,
Among the fierce acacia thorns,
You have reached the end, of your
Evolutionary road, you satisfy your needs,
Give no pain, but beautify the world,
In which you move. Your god,
If you thought of such things,
Would fill the earth with green things,
With tall grass, and with acacia trees,
And would leave the rest to you.

Rhinoceros,
Your small, black eyes,
Fixed implacably, on a blurred something,
Which could be a harmless shrub,
Or perhaps, a creeping predator,
If the first, you may eat it, in time,
If the second, it will never eat you,
While you live, secure in your
Great strength. Your god,
If you thought of such things,
Would keep his massive, horned nose,
Out, and leave you to,
Your simple life.

Lions,
Lying in sated slumber,
After the night's hunt,
As the early rays, shaft through,
The drifting mist. Your brutality has,
Its limits, dictated by a full belly,
Your god, if you thought of such things,
Would have dried blood on his chin,
And matted in the fur,
Of his breast,

Man,
Mighty, and evolved victim,
Of your own dominance.
Your god, when you think of him,
Has many names, is more ancient than time,
Is as capricious as a child,
Tells you to love one another,
And to hate those, who will not,
Accept his tender,
Doctrine.

You look,
With wondering love,
You shed a tear, in homage,
To all the miracles,
Of his creation,
And may yet,
Destroy
Them
All.

Off the Treadmill.

The other night, I dreamed that I had bought,
A ticket to the fights. The slogan said,
"Sport is our life," And then, "Our life is sport,"
That simple thought filled me with a strange dread,
In the main event, my hero, at the bell,
Bore all my aspirations. Dreams and hopes,
Stood with him when he stood, fell when he fell,
Slumped helplessly with him, against the ropes.

No matter how ferocious his attack,
No matter how guilefully he defended,
I just knew he'd end the fight, flat on his back,
Toes up, and sure enough, the boom descended,
Knowing, somehow, my fighter knocked so flat,
Was symbolic of my own pathetic life,
I mooched morosely homeward, kicked the cat,
And lost a savage fist fight, with my wife,

Alright, I knew that it was just a dream,
But I felt myself for bruises, just in case,
It had felt so real, and strange as it may seem,
There's an element of truth we all should face,
You watch soccer to relax? I guarantee,
You'll end the game more stressed than when it started,
Watch for escape? It will not set you free,
Euphoric, you may be, or broken hearted,

Free, you are not! Adrenaline has surged,
Through bulging veins, as back and forth you've reeled,
When the final whistle goes, you're on the verge,
More knackered, than if you'd been on the field.
Two mates sit down, to watch United play,
Happy as kids, out on a fairground ride,
Just ninety minutes later, both as grey,
As badgers, they're discussing suicide.

The problem is that we identify,
Part of us, is that player, on the ball,
Subconsciously, it is not "He," But "I",
Who blasts the penalty wide of the goal.
You are the British ace, whose demon serve,
Deserts him, halfway through the final set,
You, who feeling so embarrassed, and unnerved,
Throw your racket at a ball boy, in a pet,

And the crowd, whose vague suspicion, that you're crap,
Is confirmed each time you throw away your serve,
Has transferred allegiance, to the other chap,
And cheers wildly when you get what you deserve
You are the Brit, in the ten thousand metre race,
Behind all the rest, is the pacemaker too fast?
Or are you still adjusting to the pace,
When, in the final lap, you trail in last?

You are the forward, always caught in offside traps,
The England captain, piling runs up, on the board,
As you wait for the inevitable collapse,
As the, "Depleted," Aussies put you to the sword,
Sport and life, you think you're good enough to linger,
At the crease, there's nothing much to trouble you,
Out there, up goes the umpire's index finger,
You're out! Caught and bowled, or LBW.

Life and sport, how inextricably they're meshed,
Each in some ways, analogous of each,
In life, like athletes, in our England vests,
We strive always, for what is just out of reach,
When sport is in the doldrums, so are we,
Defeat becomes the norm, and breeds defeat,
But there is an answer! We can all be free,
If we only play with people we can beat!

A time to heal.

The last man choked his life out in the dust,
And there was silence,
As though the planet held its breath.
Then a sigh of wind stirred crisp fallen leaves,
Odd lights here and there, obedient to schedules,
Pre-set, by engineers long dead,
Seemed to feebly struggle,
Against the onset of night,
And darkness fell.

Black shadows turned to grey,
The sun, red in the dust haze, rose again,
There was birdsong in the roadside trees,
And on the ground, whiskers twitched,
Tiny black eyes gleamed,
And all was stir, and furtive movement,
Furry shapes moved, without fear,
Towards the shapeless bundle,
In the gutter.

The red sun rose and fell,
Bright rays speared through morning mist,
Clouds rolled around the Earth,
Wild beasts moved stealthily,
Through silent streets,
Where cars, long abandoned,
Sank to the ground, rusting slowly to ruin.
Green things crept inexorably,
Into the city,

Sycamore took root in pavement cracks,
Crows roosted in sagging roofs.
The sound of falling masonry,
Echoed in the stillness.
Seasons came and went,
Bright sun gleamed on ocean,
On mountain and river,
The virus was gone at last,
And the Earth was slowly healing.

Alternative therapies.

If you have a gyppy tummy, love,
Don't you bother with GP's,
My loveopathy clinic offers,
All the latest therapies,
Dr Me will examine you,
(May have to loosen clothes a bit.)
Laying on of hands will follow,
And the right remedy to fit,

Will be found, by trial and error,
I've found that's always the best way,
I never rush my diagnosis,
In fact, it may well take all day.
If massage is the answer, good,
We specialize in that,
Our massage couch is six feet wide,
And the clinic is in my flat.

Though some therapies we offer,
You may well think a little bold!
They're applied with tender loving care,
And our instruments are never cold,
Physio? That may be given,
One must exercise oneself,
To work up a gentle sweat, can be,
So good for a patient's health.

What are my qualifications?
Well, I seem to have lost the letter.
But I've a degree in TLC,
And a master's in kissing better.
You say I'm the only doctor,
In this practice! Can't deny it,
But then, you're the only patient,
I need the practice love, let's try it!

More Equal.

He had left him well set up, his dear Papa,
He lived in a gleaming mansion, out of town,
Rode (If he liked) In chauffeur-driven cars,
And in the season, often rode to hounds.

He dressed in suits from Savile Row, of course,
Or in waxed jackets, tweeds, and hand-made boots,
And the beaters came from his estate work force,
When he Range Rover'd out to pheasant shoots.

So, he was filthy rich, was he content?
Not on your life, he simply wanted more,
He had built a brand-new factory, in Kent,
Where Daddy had bought a run-down hardware store.

They made hand-luggage, handbags, gloves, and shoes,
The leather came from beasts on the estate,
His researchers told him," John, you just can't lose,
There's need, out there, for all that you can make."

The world was in recession, John was pleased,
Rubbing his hands, as firms went to the wall,
He spoke to agents of the Japanese,
Germans, and Swedes, he bought a shopping mall.

Though trade was gone, the buildings were ok,
The biggest of them, suited, to a tee,
The smaller ones were perfect, by the way,
For selling products from his other factory,

He leased the rest, to tradesmen from the town,
At half the rent the council had imposed,
Drive out there now, you'll find, I'll bet a pound,
It's hard to park! The place is never closed,

"Footfall," he says, with enigmatic smile,
His shops awash with punters, who work hard,
To give themselves the best, to live in style,
John thanks his stars for all those credit cards.

But in his car component works, he's really blessed,
Dinero rolling in from every side,
Has bought a yacht marina, in the west,
A flat, in Mayfair, for his lovely bride.

But for his millions, would she have hung on?
Have stuck around? It's difficult to say,
It's said, before she zeroed in on John,
Two strikers, and a pop star were in play.

It was on "Question Time", that he was caught,
By a man, who had been his nemesis for years,
Red, of the Union, said, "Just had a thought,
When are you going to pay your tax arrears?"

"Five thousand men, who've helped you buy your yacht,
Are all paying twenty pence for every pound,
Do you really feel no guilt, at what you've got?
Or the pocket change, you pay back to the crown?"

"You're wrong, of course," Said John, "I pay my dues,
The tax inspector has no doubts at all,
But if I ever need an audit, Red, then you,
My friend, would be the last man I would call."

Said Red, "You've built a fortune on the sweat,
Of better men than you could ever be,
And never will acknowledge the great debt,
Your kind will always owe to such as me."

"Your creed," said John, "Is to apportion blame,
And to resent the strides that others make,
Let us be clear, not all men are the same,
Treat them as such, you make a big mistake,

If what you call, "My kind," Had never been,
How then, Red, would you feed your family?
It saddens me to say, to you who dreams,
Of a utopia of true equality,

Read your history, you will be a wiser man!
My factories pay five thousand men a wage,
Paid holidays, a health insurance plan,
And every one a pension, in old age."

"Who is the better, who the lesser? Well,
That is not the issue. You may not agree,
But my covenants will sink a thousand wells,
My covenants will plant a million trees.

"My greed," As you have named it many times,
Sends British products all around the earth,
"My greed," is building factories, in the North,
Where four in every ten, are seeking work.

I took a small fortune, and made a bit,
That's true., but there are better men, by far,
Who with no more than application, flair, and grit,
Have come to where I am, from where you are."

You think that only poor men should be free,
You have made the rich the object of your hate,
This world is not as you would have it be,
Open your eyes, before it is too late,"

Mad Moggie.

"The British league of feline friends,"
Said the sign beside the door,
And once inside, it was the end,
Of a feline's friend we saw,
As she bent, to pick up, from the mat,
A feline she'd befriended,
It was hard to say just where the cat,
Began, and where she ended.

No one could doubt that she must love,
Or that her love was true,
Inside, her house reminds you of,
The cat- house at the zoo.
She wore an old black top, threadbare,
An ancient pair of slacks,
And stuck to both, more moggie hair,
Than stuck out of her cats.

As I viewed this fashion statement,
In her house, scraped free of paint,
Who to cats, hurt and forsaken,
Was a kind of patron saint,
My wife gazed round the battle zone,
As one completely smitten,
And I knew, that when we went back home,
We would have at least one kitten.

But the cat we took back home with us,
Was the ugliest in the place,
I half believed a toilet brush,
Which had seen better days,
Looked up at us, with one green eye,
(The other eye was blue.)
Ellie crooned, "Don't oo wowwy boy,
Mommy ook after oo."

I moaned, "Of all the cats she had,
Why pick this travesty?"
She smiled that smile, "He looked so sad,
I knew he needed me."
I knew I shouldn't be surprised,
She chose that little ball,
Of matted fur, and miss- matched eyes,
She chose me, after all!

I think I could have coped with that,
But she just had to say,
"Think darling, he's the sort of cat,
No one will steal away."
You know, that sort of chance remark,
Can make a man's mind active.
Did I attract her, at the start,
By being unattractive?

From then, until we went to bed,
We played a silly game,
"We can't just call him "Cat" she said,
 He has to have a name,"
Ellie, of literary bent,
Chose "Homer" and "Voltaire",
When I said "Cyclops Two" she sent,
Me such a withering stare.

I tried "Frankenstein" though she,
Was not too keen on that,
But I said, "He's made, it seems to me,
From bits of other cats.
For every aspect of the brute,
Betrayed its ancestry,
It clearly was the fallen fruit,
Of a tangled family tree,

Each donor, to that muddy pool,
Had left its little mark,
His hair was short, his hair was long,
His hair was light, and dark,
Around his neck, a ginger tom,
Had left an orange frill,
A tabby's stripes, circled his bum,
Which moved when he sat still,

His ears were longer than a bat's,
And shivered in the breeze,
A Persian's head, while at the back,
A hint of Siamese,
While one eye stared in dumb distress,
The other winked, in sport,
And the tail. Protruding from this mess,
Was like an afterthought.

The kitten, rolling on the mat,
Playing his kitten's games,
Was moggie, head to toe, and that,
Was how he got his name.
But from the day that Mog arrived,
He ate the choicest fare,
He lived in luxury, and thrived,
On tender, loving care.

For my Ellie has more love than most,
More than enough to spare,
She bought him bowls, and scratching posts,
She groomed his tangled hair,
She lay with him, down on the mat,
She stroked him, tenderly,
At times, I thought the lousy cat,
Meant more, to her, than me.

But when the cat was fully grown,
Well, awesome, was the word,
The monarch of our little home,
To whom we both deferred,
He wore a coat, of many hues,
Grey, brown, black, blue, and red,
The long ears were a British Blue's,
Set on that Persian head,

His orange mane, Tom's legacy,
Flowed, in a silken frill,
While round his bum, those tabby stripes,
That moved when he sat still.
And over that substantial rear,
Waving triumphantly,
That long and bushy tail was clearly,
All a tail should be.

A dusky black moustache was curled,
Above his bearded chin,
His blue- green eyes surveyed the world,
With a satyr's leering grin.
With us, in the house by day,
He was his mummy's boy,
In gentle Ellie's lap, he lay,
A living cuddly toy.

But slipping through the flap, at night,
His other self took over,
No concept, now, of wrong or right,
A pirate, and a rover,
He stalked the shadowed alleyways,
A creature, wild and free,
In that night world, of blues and greys,
He knew no boundary.

Few movements, in the shifting shade,
Escaped his shining eye,
And in the dark, no sound betrayed,
The hunter passing by.
A sense of forebears, in a time,
When all the land was free,
And long-dead hunters of his line,
Stirred, like a memory.

Looking to kill, or love, or fight,
His blood at fever heat,
Ears at the stretch, he stalked the night,
On silent padding feet,
Few toms, met in his nightly tours,
Forgot him easily,
Few queens, who had not felt the force,
Of his virility.

His victims lay out, on the step,
Or just inside the fence,
At break of day, while Moggie slept,
The sleep of innocence.
To see him, drowsing on the mat,
Or in his favourite chair,
You could believe the lazy cat,
Had spent the whole night there.

Our neighbour had a shaggy hound,
He called a collie cross,
Jim smirked, "Of all the dogs around,
Old Satan is the boss."
He warned me, "Keep that cat inside,
And under lock and key,
'Or if old Satan has his hide,
Don't put the blame on me."

And every day, from early dawn,
The gruesome dog ran free,
Making it plain, he viewed my lawn,
As his private lavatory,
For nothing stood in Satan's way,
In his world, he was king,
How could he know he'd meet, that day,
His day of reckoning?

He stalked my land, and could not miss,
With his unerring eye,
He squirted everything, from his,
Unlimited supply,
Then stood awhile, beneath a tree,
Still making up his mind,
Where he would leave the gift, for me,
He always left behind.

To see our cat, pacing along,
In through the garden gate,
Set Satan's pulses racing on,
He would not hesitate,
With every filament of hair,
Erect, along his back,
His fearsome baying rent the air,
Satan, On the attack!

Moggie knew he must fight, or flee,
The only choice, was war,
Between him, and the nearest tree,
A raving carnivore.
I saw, in the ensuing fray,
Between the hound, and Mog,
Just what it means, when people say,
"They fought, like cat and dog."

The embattled feline's fearful squalls,
The baying of the hound,
Reverberated round the walls,
A horrid wall of sound,
While on the path, a bristling ball,
Of multi-coloured fur,
Leapt, screeching, through the air, to fall,
On the onrushing cur.

Their wild melee tore up the grass,
And flowers in their way,
That Satan was out of his class,
With Mog, was clear as day,
He fought a brave rear-guard defence,
But knew when he was beaten,
He hurled himself back through the fence,
(It was that or be eaten!)

Satan has never ventured in,
My garden since that day.
Whenever Moggie strolled past him,
He 'd quietly slink away,
He had learned a lesson, that's for sure,
And was the better for it,
Not so his boss, the man was sore,
No way would he ignore it!

And sure enough, the angry tough,
Came banging at my door,
And by his foot, the shredded mutt,
Lay cowering, on the floor,
In Jimmy's mind, a cat of mine,
Had minced a dog of his,
He had to pay me back in kind,
By giving me some fist.

I suppose it's logic, of a sort,
Beloved of louts and toughs,
And as his ghastly dog had thought,
He knew he'd see me off,
But suddenly, I was inspired,
By what I had seen that day,
I told him that he made me tired,
And would he "Go away."

I must have had a rush of blood,
For then, I said to Jim,
What his dog had learned that day, I would,
Be glad to teach to him.
To my surprise, I saw him flinch,
I couldn't help but smile,
I never thought he'd give an inch,
But I'd taken a mile.

Who would think, when we took Moggie in,
That he would change my life?
Give me the strength and will to win,
To triumph over strife.
I've learned to meet the world, head on.
Nobody puts me down,
I owe him everything I've won,
But Moggie is not around!

Yes, Moggie's gone. Yet still lives on,
For, in his favourite chair,
Sits Cyclops Two, eyes green, and blue,
And multi-coloured hair,
Down on the mat, another cat,
Built to the same design,
Eyes blue, and green, the same mad grin,
His brother, Frankenstein.

Sam Sand's Shining Summer.

Scene:
Scarborough Sands,
Summer, seventy-seven,
Sweltering sunshine,
Several sweaty seaside shoppers,
(Simple souls) Seeking some shade,
Sit shattered, slowly sipping squash.
Samuel Sands, seed salesman,
Standing stiffly, somewhat shy,
Saw sweet Susie Smith, sitting,
Sombre, silent.

Sam, seeing She seemed,
Somehow slightly sad, said,
"Susie - saw some super shades,"
(Sun spectacles sometimes sent Susie silly)
She seemed strangely somnolent,
"Sorry Sam," she said, "Sunglasses?"
Sam shuffled, started speaking,
Stumblingly, stammering, "S - Susie,"
Susie sighed, "Sam, surely sweethearts,
Should show some sign."

Sam sat suddenly,
"Sweethearts?" Said Sam, staring,
Susie smiled sweetly,
"Say something, Sam," she said simply.
"Sweet Susie," Said Sam, shaking,
"Somewhere, sometime soon,
Shimmering silver stars shall shine,
Saying, "Susie Smith, Sam Sands,
Sweethearts."

Seven sensational sunny Summers,
Swiftly spent. Samuel Sands,
Successful seaside shopkeeper,
Slightly stoned, sleeps soundly,
Snuffling, softly snoring,
Susie Sands, still smiling sweetly,
Sits sewing Sammy's school socks,
Sammy Sands, seven,
Sits, silently studying,

Sindy Sands,
Sammy's small sister,
Sings silly songs.

More questions than answers.

You know how much I care for you,
Why must you tell such lies?
"Sorry my love, it's such a pain,
I'm working extra shifts again,
I'll see you Monday, on the train,"
Why am I not surprised?

"Together darling, we're so good,"
Remember you said that?
All those lovely things you said,
That rattle round inside my head,
Were they just to get me into bed?
Why am I such a prat?

You're somewhere else when you're with me,
I've seen it in your eyes,
Last week, when I was at your place,
And the phone rang, I saw your face,
You said it was your sister Grace,
Then took the phone outside.

And yes, I've seen you sneaking looks,
At your watch, when we're talking,
Am I taking up your precious time?
Could you really think that I'm so blind?
Love, I don't need to have a mind,
You know, like Steven Hawking.

To see the writing on the wall,
It might as well be neon,
In letters eighteen inches high,
"Yes dear, there goes another lie,"
You would be Pope, if pigs could fly,
What planet could you be on?

But perhaps I'm being hard on you,
Nobody's perfect, right?
You've lots of pressure in your life,
No fun to have a frigid wife,
With a tongue, that's sharper than a knife,
I'll call you back tonight!

The Double- Glazing Rep.

He tramps from door to door, the live-long day,
His face wreathed in ingratiating smiles,
His sprightly step belies the weary way,
Those aching feet have travelled, or the miles,
To where the little house, on Grange Estate,
Stands, mortgaged to the hilt, where his sweet wife,
Embodiment of dreams, his true soul mate,
Sharing the aspirations of his life,
Has held him in her arms, and with the dawn,
He has sallied forth, as some bold knight of old,
To face the fearsome foe, with hope reborn,
Armed, with the warmth of love against the cold.

Jehovah's witnesses don't want to talk,
To him, bores find him boring, brave men cringe,
Behind their sofas, when they see him walking,
Up the path. Insurance salesmen whinge,
"Oh, not another!" Vicars coldly stare,
Samaritans feel suicidal urges,
Pacifists rage, optimists, in despair,
Abandon hope, the moment he emerges,
Out of his car, the cheerful smile in place,
Old men on Zimmer walkers, sprint away,
To double-lock their front door, just in case,
His is a game that no one wants to play.

Faced daily as he is, with raw aggression,
Seeing his tireless efforts brought to naught,
He will not give in to rancour, or depression,
But positive his every waking thought,
Sows countless seeds, that one may see fruition,
Cajoles, advises, never will insist,
From nine to five, living but for his mission,
This driving force, this born evangelist,
Show me the man, who striving for his goal,
Can smile at cold indifference, and hate,
I will show you, in that one resilient soul,
The spirit which made this great nation great.

Sights for sore eyes.

I have seen the Acropolis,
The many beauties of Versailles
The sun, over Kilimanjaro,
Rise into a roseate sky,
The Parthenon, the Taj Mahal,
Beneath a summer moon,
The Pyramids of Giza,
Well, we shall see them soon.

And I have seen you, darling,
Come to the bedroom, so aware,
Of the hungry eyes that watch you,
With a predatory stare,
Of all the stirring sights I've seen
To me, by far the best,
Is to see my lovely woman,
When she comes to me,
Undressed.

Voices.

As Joan of Orleans did (It's said)
I can hear voices in my head.
They tell me how, and why, and who,
What clothes to wear, and what to do,
Strange and mysterious sounds I hear,
Borne through the ether to my ear,
Though I hide in a darkened room,
And crouch, unseen, within the gloom,
Still these strange voices around me play,
Though those who speak, are far away.

I hear them when the sun is bright,
Or in the very dead of night,
They prattle at me endlessly,
In chatty, crass inanity,
Not everyone's idea of fun,
Yet doggedly, I listen on,
I listen, though I'm quite incensed,
Just searching for one grain of sense.
You minions of the BBC,
What hold is this you have on me?

A man from Ireland, and a Scot,
Both talking the same brand of rot,
Yet through their guff, a thread of wit,
A joke or two that's worth a titter,

Adds seasoning to all the hype,
And almost undiluted tripe,
Which they indulge in, on their "progs"
To quote old Jimmy Young, whose cogs,
Begin to creak a bit, of late,
The hair grows thinner on the pate,

But then, he's been around a while,
You can be sure, he's made his pile,
For Jim, you know, was once a singer,
An idol, heartthrob, and a swinger,
Gay and romantic, and all that,
Who young girls threw their knickers at,
And from Jim's show, sometimes, some sense,
Is broadcast through the elements,
He gets some telling points across,
Jim's show is not a total loss.

One thing that really knocks me aback,
When that man Wogan makes a crack,
Someone, somewhere far away,
A prisoner doing porridge, say,
In Strangeways, or in Wormwood Scrubs,
Or one of those gentlemen's clubs,
Lying idly scratching, on his bunk,
In apathetic daydreams sunk,
Will come to elbow on his truckle,
And raise his shaggy head to chuckle.

While in Buck House, our gracious Queen,
Seated on cushions velveteen.
Her carefully coiffed head will wag,
And laugh as merry as the lag,
Deep dungeoned in that prison pile,
And smile a simultaneous smile,
She calls out, to her escort, Phil,
Stood glowering at the windowsill,
Thinking of what kind words to say,
At the next Buck House open day,

What cheering message for the folk,
(He is a diplomatic bloke)
She calls out, as I say, " Philip,
Did you hear that merry quip?
He is a wit, that Irish chappie."
Says Philip, "It would make me happy,
To see the bugger sent from hence,
I would greatly value his absence,
Back to that boggy, emerald land,
And let him join a ceilidh band,

They're taking jobs the English seek."
Queen, (Wondering) "Could he be Greek?
As the queen, in her fine parlour,
And the old felon in his squalor,
The Scottish parson, in his manse,
Is hitching at the frilly pants,

Under the parson's clothes he wears,
When Wogan's voice floats up the stairs,
He really can't suppress a grin,
As he tucks his half -slip in,

A good man, though unsure of gender,
He tightens up a slack suspender,
And stands awhile, before the glass,
While with his cape, he makes a pass,
Then casting a flirtatious glance,
The holy man begins to dance,
Performs an arabesque, fantastic,
With many a twang of pink elastic,
Then in his sober parson's weeds,
He sallies forth to plant some seeds.

The young bride, married for a week,
Leans to the window for a peek,
Across the gardens, up the lane,
And thinks of going home again,
To where her mum would make her tea,
She'd sit upon her father's knee,
And never have to scrub the floor,
Or wash the dishes, what a bore!
Or do the washing, hang it out,
Or carry all that coal about.

Or stagger up the street with shopping,
Bloody housework, till she's dropping,
She feels a tear squeeze from her eye.
"You've made your bed; on it you'll lie."
Comes Wogan's blarney from the shelf,
She has to laugh, in spite of self,
Laughs with her disembodied friend,
Borne through the ether, on the wind,
Then tells herself she must be mad!
And yet she doesn't feel so bad.

What truly awesome power this medium,
Has, that it can relieve the tedium,
Of convict, lifer, doing time,
For some grim, antisocial crime,
Or cheer the parson, in his frills,
As he goes out to right some ills.
So radio for me, a pox,
I say, upon the goggle box.
When I say that, don't be misled,
I haven't quite gone off my head,

When listening to the BBC,
I still retain my sanity,
If you'd hang on to yours as well,
Then listen to the tale I tell.

Though fools may say its harmless fun,
Never get hooked on Radio One,
Its dangers can't be overstated,
A chap with ego so inflated,
Thinking himself some sort of toff will,
Bombard the eardrum with his waffle,

And dress himself and wife in mink,
While driving sober men to drink,
So now the dried- out alcoholic,
Sits listening, doubled up with colic,
Then staggers outside, in the rain,
And gets completely pissed again,
Easy to see why he would do it,
The poor slob has been driven to it!
And what gets me into such rages,
We are the ones who pay their wages.

Who wants them, tell me that, who needs them?
They bite the very hand that feeds them.
It must be said, you take a risk,
Intrepid jockeys of the disc
To move among the cognoscente.
With heads made vacuous and empty,
By deejays who must fill each gap,
With endless reams of puerile crap,
Dark vacant eyes with reddened rims,
Slack mouths spread in demented grins,

They've taken far too much Blackburn,
They're past the point of no return,
They are on the brink, they've had enough,
Their reeling brains are stuffed with Fluff,
They shamble, aimless, round the town,
Carry their babies upside down,
And for them, round each corner waits,
An eldritch, grinning Simon Bates.
One of these days (The thought is ghastly)
A crowd of them may just turn nasty,

Grab the manic, cheery Tone,
And make him eat his microphone,
With awful cries of, "Now, you prat,
Let us see you make a joke of that."
Or strap a headset on Ed Stewart,
Then play tapes of Mick Jagger through it,
Turning the volume knob up high,
Then watch him, with a cunning eye,
Until his eyes begin to roll,
His mouth becomes a ragged hole.

Shrill screams of anguish fill the air,
He falls back, with a vacant stare,
Then starts to talk, his tone is bland,
He says things none can understand,
I've heard brainwashing can be grim,
But it's made no bloody odds to him!

I have a vision, so heartrending,
Of strange wild figures, apprehending,
Every man beneath the sun,
Who ever worked for Radio One,

Then heedless of their piteous cries,
Their flailing arms, their streaming eyes,
Drag them kicking, yes and screaming,
To where, with red eyes madly gleaming,
Wait groups of Radio One fanatics,
Who take and lock them up in attics,
Where endlessly they rave and chatter,
Of things that simply do not matter,
And driven by their own addresses,
To paroxysms, and wild excesses,

They dash about, they rise and fall,
They bash themselves against the wall,
Till with the unrelenting gloom,
Incarcerated in one room,
Begin to talk like normal men,
Are fit to be let out again,
To walk abroad, unfettered, free,
Take their place in society,
And never again, as once they had,
Drive any poor sad bugger mad.

Rufus black.

Rufus Black, I knew him well,
A gentle man, in many ways,
When I was just a little girl,
Granddad and I shared golden days,
A slight man, and of no great size,
But bigger men than he stood back,
From what they saw in those dark eyes,
Which said, "Don't mess with Rufus Black.

For sure, he took life as it came,
But I saw him once, touched on the raw,
That day, he lived up to his name,
Rufus was red, in tooth and claw.
A fierce dog roamed the district then,
With snapping jaw, and rolling eye,
Who simply loved the legs of men,
Be it buttock, ankle, calf or thigh.

As he came, weary from the field, the hound,
Lurched from the trees, savage and bold,
Pitching old Rufus to the ground,
As those white canines took a hold,
Two sinewy arms, two horny hands,
Seized the dog fast, and pulled him in,
He saw the flash of two long fangs,
And felt them meet, beneath his skin.

Rufus had two teeth of his own,
Two shards like daggers, from the gum,
Sank through fur and flesh, down to the bone,
And the dog ran, as he'd never run.
From that day, when he saw men grin,
Their white teeth gleaming, in the sun,
He would feel those teeth sink through his skin,
And shuddering, would think of one,
A sturdy soul named Rufus Black,
A man he bit, who bit him back.

Loving friends.

You say I'm coming on too strong.
I see the sense in what you're saying,
You say, surely, we must be friends,
Before we think of being lovers,
Well good for you, you are not wrong,
This is a long- term game we're playing,
They say the opera doesn't end,
Till the fat lady sings her song.

Yes! Let's be mates, let's be best buddies,
It should be fun, what shall we do?
To prove how much we like each other.
Just let me think. Yes, we could go,
Out shopping, and buy lots of goodies,
Have wrestling matches (No, that won't do.)
Just think of me as your big brother.
Yes, that's good, I'll take you to the zoo.

And when we go out in the evening,
We'll walk back, scoffing fish and chips,
And have a friendly hug, at parting,
That's okay, mates often do that.
I may just kiss you, when you're leaving,
But never ever on the lips,
We could ski, we could go go-Karting,
That should be good. I'll tell you what!

We could watch adventures, in the cinema,
Where Arnie decimates his foes,
With a rocket launcher, blasts their asses,
(He's carried it, just in case it's needed)
Or watch James Bond do something similar,
Firing a death ray down his nose,
From a pair of artificial glasses.
Your arm on mine, will go unheeded.

After all, you're just my best mate. Right?
Though sometimes, pal, I may want to hold you,
And whisper sweet things to my chum,
And kiss my friend's face, if I may,
And hold my mate's hand, in the night,
And in my friendly arms, enfold you,
And maybe, stroke my buddy's bum,
'Cos when you're lovers, that's okay.

The used car dealer.

I bought myself a car, when I was young,
All gleaming paint, and chrome, and glass, although,
What points, and tappets are, I never knew,
I'm not too sure today, to tell the truth,
Yet I knew, even when I was a youth,
Though life can be a jungle, there are few,
More useful attributes, than just to know,
The ways of men, I seldom got it wrong.

I saw at once, the salesman was friend,
His red face beaming, and his honest eyes,
Told me, here was a man that I could trust,
He warned me, to beware of dealers who,
Wound clocks back, and he warned me too,
Of fresh new paint, sprayed over ,"Heaps of rust."
"Not me," He said, "But if I told you lies,
Your warranty would protect you, in the end."

As happy as a puppy with two tails,
With my new passport to the adult world,
I drove to town, to casually cruise around,
Stealing a march, on all my wheel-less mates.
The day was bright and warm, I felt the fates,
Were on my side, I wound my window down,
Feeling suavely irresistible to girls,
One of those handsome, predatory males.

The grinding sound, as I drove through the town,
"Wheel bearings bedding in," My mentor said,
"Why does it cough and splutter, when it starts?"
"High performance engine, highly tuned,
It's self-adjusting, it'll settle soon."
Then came the awful day that broke my heart,
For while I slept, my pride and joy had spread,
A massive pool of oil, upon the ground.

Three months had gone, the gilt was wearing thin,
As was the winsome charm of "Honest John,"
He said, "You've got a problem there, no doubt,
The clutch is gone, the gearbox too, I'd say,
Now don't be silly, you know I can't pay,
I'd like to, but your warranty is out,
Your luck is in though son, for just a ton,
I know a chap, who'll put a new clutch in."

I thought of the fat toad's unsavoury tricks,
Of how my simple trust had been abused,
My confidence won with a nod and wink,
How, even while he planned to do me harm,
He'd oozed with matey flattery, and smarm,
Why should I view his blotchy face, and think,
In a distracted way, (I was confused),
Of politicians, and of politics?

Paradise Confiscated.

West of Nod, a sylvan vale of heavenly light,
Basked in the golden sun of a new world,
Where lived a man, and there for his delight,
Bright flowers would bloom, and trees festooned with
birds,
Of gorgeous hue, for this was God's own garden,
Planted by him, when heaven and earth were one,
For this one perfect man, who was its warden,
And was made by he who made the very sun.

Bright crystal pools there were, for him to bathe in,
And mossy winding paths, where he could walk,
The creator, when he took breaks from creating,
Walked with the perfect man, and they would talk,
This man, of course, who knew the tongue of angels,
Was never a babe, had never learned to cry,
Bursting from a mote of nothing, to perfection,
In much less than the twinkling of an eye.

And there was nothing in his world to pain him,
No thorns or brambles grew in that sweet land,
When he was hungry, good fruit, to sustain him,
Would ripen, at the reaching of his hand.
"Adam," said God, as they walked in the evening,
"You're sad." "No Lord, what, in this paradise?"
It would be churlish of me to be grieving."
But God had seen a shadow in his eye,

"Adam, would you like someone here, to live with?
A woman?" Adam said, "Sounds good to me,
But Lord, what is this thing, a woman?"
Said God, "Just go to sleep, my son, you'll see."
When he awoke, God was gone, but by his side,
In the soft grass, lay something so unreal,
It hurt his chest, it brought tears to his eyes,
Such pain, such joy, such wonder, did he feel.

He knew at once, his life, until that day,
Had been pale shadows of what it could be,
She opened glistening eyes, and looked his way,
"Adam," She whispered, "Man, do you want me?"
This beauteous thing, he knew, was Eve, his woman,
They worked and played together, laughed, and loved,
And when God came to them, they heard him coming,
Like a mighty rushing wind, somewhere above,

"This is your home," Said God, "Through all the seasons,
Here, you will live in joy, eternally,
I will tell you now, my rules, but not my reasons,
Eat what you will, except for that one tree."
And after God had left, Adam said, "Pardon?
God's little pets shared smiles of disbelief,
"A single tree," Said Eve, "From all this garden/"
"Hard work," said Adam, laughing with relief.

And God heard every word, he'd always known,
The secrets of all things in his creation,
A serpent slithered, where bright fruit had grown,
He smiled ca smile of quiet anticipation,
He knew what was to come, he is omniscient,
And when they fell, he raged, that was his way,
"Exile, pain, death," He roared, "Is that sufficient?
The Lord giveth, the Lord taketh away."

First love.

I knew a little girl,
She was the only one,
Her eyes were blue as cornflowers,
Her teeth were pearls,
Her hair a mass of curls,
Shone like the morning sun,
Her nose was a pert button,
She was such a girl.

With such a smile,
She held my hand in hers,
I felt such joy,
The stirring of true love,
In all its glory,
She was my little girl,
I was her little boy,
Then she ate all my Smarties.
End of story.

Darkness.

The dark. I used to be afraid,
Of darkness, I would hide my head,
Thinking some thing crept up on me,
To touch me, as I lay in bed,
If something creaked, or curtains quivered,
I simply did not want to see,
Be honest now, who has not shivered,
And feared the threatening dark, like me?

I have a different slant, these nights,
On darkness, feelings make me shake,
Wouldn't exactly call it fright,
Though it certainly keeps me awake,
Of course, I mean when you are there,
Then Old Darkness is a friend of mine,
If I reach out, to stroke your hair,
Or something, that is so divine,

Can't see single thing in here,
Well frankly, I don't mind it much.
I can still whisper in your ear,
We can still communicate by touch,
Since you've been mine, I have to say,
The day has lost some of its charm,
I find I chafe at the delay,
Want darkness, and you in my arms.

How do they do that?

Have you ever seen shire horses?
How the ground shakes, when they pass,
Can it be true, those giants grew,
From eating leaves and grass?
Or take the mighty elephant,
Even harder to believe,
I tell no lies, he got that size,
From eating grass and leaves,

Those herds of mighty wildebeest,
Sweeping across the plain,
So big, so fleet. What do they eat?
Why, grass and leaves again.
What of the brontosaurus?
What fulfilled its massive needs?
Life was a feast, for this great beast,
Head down, among the weeds.

Think of a cow. Please tell me how,
She packs on so much mass,
For her, its worse, she must get hers,
From eating grass, and grass,
Compared to such efficiency,
We are the poor relation,
So, I suppose, we must eat those,
Who eat the vegetation.

Why not eat grass?" I hear you ask,
"Those other creatures do it,
We could as well." No, truth to tell,
We are just not suited to it,
Our teeth would grind down to the rind,
Devoid of all dentition,
Our backs would bend, our fronts distend,
We'd die of malnutrition!

Meet me tonight.

Standing in the icy wind, I looked along the street,
And turned by back, against the driving rain,
Still looking for the memory I had arranged to meet,
The sweet memory, who shared my greatest moment of
defeat,
And who I'd doubted I would ever see again.
She was a woman then, who had a lot to give,
And God knows why, she gave it all to me,
I was temptations pawn, back then, and leaky as a sieve,
I threw it all away, and for as long as I shall live,
I will know just what a fool a man can be.

"Easy come, easy go", That's what I used to say,
I thought myself the master of my fate,
Things did come easily to me, I took, that was my way,
And devil take the rest, till it's too late.
The bitter hurt I gave her long ago, the pain,
I still recall in those dark gentle eyes,
I had been a faithless lover, but never would again,
I gave her tears and promises, it was all in vain,
The truth I told was lost in all my lies.

Its fair, that, old and grey, I wait for her, who long ago,
Would wait for me, playing my foolish games,
And fair that I must hope and pray, if only she will show,
She will never want for tender love again, and yes, I
know,
It's only fair, that in the end, she never came.

Kango, Don, and Will.

What gets you from your bed each day,
With a spring in your step, and a grin?
When common sense tells you to stay,
With the duvet pulled up to your chin.

It is the triumph of hope over doubt,
The victory of maybe over never,
When you pull back the blinds, looking out,
For sunshine, when you must know the weather,

Is going to be rain, hail, or sleet,
And a wind to cut through you with ease,
Your spirit will not own defeat,
Though the snow may be up to your knees.

Common sense, hard work, presence of mind,
Though such qualities serve a man well,
Foolish dreams are what brought humankind,
From the cave to the Hilton Hotel.

Will Ittwurk says, "I think I can fly!
I've worked out a plan, and it's sound."
Don Bedaft says, "Well and good, have a try,
As for me, I'll stay here on the ground."

And then, when poor Will breaks his neck,
Jumping out with his wings, from a tree,
Don shrugs, saying, "Well, what the heck,
The fool wouldn't listen to me."

But then, Kango Ronge comes along,
Saying, "Don my old friend, do you know?
I can see where William went wrong,
Says Don, "So now you'll have a go."

All too soon, Ronge's fame went around,
The whole world, it was in all the papers,
How he plunged head- first, into the ground,
From one of those brand-new skyscrapers!

If you think of this life as a tune,
Don played his to a sensible rhythm,
But when Kango's son walked on the moon,
Ittwurk's grandson was there with him.

Falling.

Where do our minds go when we are sleeping?
Last night, I dreamed that I was falling,
Endlessly, across a sun-bright heaven,
And all around, were others falling,
Numberless, countless, leaves in Autumn,
Further than the eye could see them.

Little children, swooping, playing,
Laughing with the joy of living,
Men called greetings to each other,
Loving mothers held their babies,
Falling lovers clung together,
Kissed and embraced, as they were falling.

Riding the warm wind that bore us,
Through skies of unearthly beauty,
We fell past bright glistening cities,
Built on hills of white cloud, shining,
Golden plains, and verdant forests,
Lakes of crystal water gleaming.

And there, for a while, I lingered,
Swam the lakes, and walked the forests,
Came to know the city's secrets,
Every corner, every alley,
Found friends aplenty, and one lover,
Dearer to me, than dreams of heaven.

And though for years, we walked together,
Somehow, I knew, we still were falling,
Through the cloud wrack, ever faster,
Falling, into mist and shadow,
Yet through the dark, something was gleaming,
Shining through the swirling blackness.

Mite and mane.

He was a handsome figure of a dust mite,
She was a most attractive dust mitess,
He asked, "Might you be mine?" She said, "I just might,
I might do a lot worse; I must confess."
"Darling," He said, "Your shade of grey- it's just right,
And I love those cheeky bristles on your bum,
I am bound for a long journey, and I must fight,
For every millimetre, will you come?"

"I ought to give you more time to adjust, bite,
My head off if you like, I have to know."
I'm heading for the double bed or bust. Light,
Is failing, and I really have to go."
She smiled, "Dear me, that is a little rushed, tight,
Your schedule may be, I shall have to see."
Surely you don't expect me to be pushed, sight,
Unseen, to join you in your fantasy."

"I'm sorry if I seem a little up tight,
But that bedroom carpet is so deep and wide."
He sighed, "This really is a bitter cup, light,
Won't seem so bright without you by my side."
She blushed, "I never saw a finer, more august mite,
And if a mite is right, to me that counts."
I think I fell in love with you at fust sight,"
(Excited mites, will often mispronounce)

"You seem the kind of mite a girl can trust.
Right! I will be your companion, and your friend,
I may be very small, but I'm robust.
Quite the mite to be your helpmite to the end."
"I never thought that I could have such luck,"
Mite cried, "My pulse is beating like a hammer,
Oh, cupid's dart! I think my heart has took flight,
(They are also prone to the odd lapse in grammar)

Then, sad to say, the two gave way to lust,
Night was falling, and beneath the easy chair,
She was wondering, did she jump, or was she pushed,
Mite was running tender feelers through her hair,
When, right out of the blue, a massive puss, white,
And fluffy, crashed down, like an avalanche,
His bristling mane, like a giant brush, wiped,
Them from the rug, before they had a chance.

Mite cried, "My love, we're heading for a rough night,"
Asa the clung together in the shaggy frill,
She whispered, "We're in luck, just snuggle up tight,
And let this pussy take us where he will,""
So, they used the giant moggie as a bus, like,
Two tourist mites, they clung among the hair,
"Let's just enjoy the journey, and not fuss,
Hike we could, but puss is sure to take us there."

They were under the duvet, she said, "It's just right,
Look around us, all those heavenly skin-scales."
"What luck," He gasped. She smiled, "No love, not luck,
Mite and mane, my intuition never fails."
And so was born a little baby dust mite,
Perfection, from his bristles to his claws,
Said Mite, "could there ever be a more joyous sight?
One day dust mite, this just might all be yours."

Two bad dads. (1)

Stan a. k. a, and other stories.

My name is Stan, and I'm a man,
Who will never be an also-ran,
I'm my own boss, don't give a toss,
If you don't like me, that's no loss,
Sure as you're born, the day won't dawn,
When I'll go out to mow the lawn,

My missus wishes I'd wash the dishes,
Like other poor pathetic fishes,
She's got a hope! She'll have to cope,
She once thought me the kind of dope,
Who'd clean the room, or wield a broom,
But now she sings another tune.

For, don't you see? Men must be free.
 That was my dad's philosophy,
He told me then, when I was ten,
"I don't mean women, I mean men,
For girls are sweet enough to eat,
But watch them, or they'll have you beat!

A communist, a pragmatist,
Bust most of all, a realist,
That was my dad, some thought him bad,
I've even heard them call him mad.
 Give them their due, I thought so too,

But much of what he said, proved true.
He was a chap who took no crap,
I very often got a slap,
A sudden flick, perhaps a kick,
He used to say I made him sick,
In the yard, chopping, or doing the mopping,
Or going into town, for shopping.

One day, he said, "Now listen, Ted,"
That's how he got into my head,
Ted's not my name, but all the same,
It was just part of my dad's game,
The evil swine, to undermine,
And make the little bugger pine.

"Get me a beer, and come over here,
Your old dad's going to bend your ear,
Take my advice, don't be so nice!
It's something I won't tell you twice.
Your mum's in there, sat in a chair,
With loads of curlers in her hair,

Smoking a fag, the lazy bag.
Living with her has become a drag,
It makes me ill, I tell you, Bill,
I don't believe she ever will,
Be worth her salt. It's all your fault,
I really could half kill you, Walt."

This may seem odd, but I swear to God,
  I was a cheeky little sod,
Bad language too, my tongue was blue,
It often dropped me in the poo,
"My mom is weak? You've got a cheek,
I said, "You've done fuck-all for weeks."

A big arm, bare, except for hair,
Came whistling through the stilly air,
It landed, smack, and knocked me back,
I landed like an empty sack,
Under the wringer, it was a stinger,
I felt the print of every finger.

"Believe it or not, that mouth you've got,
One day, it's going to get you shot."
I looked up then, and that was when,
He bent, and helped me up again,
Then he went on, "As I said, Ron,
It's you who are the guilty one,"

"You hear her bawl, and that is all,
It takes, to make you start to crawl,
For your own sake I warn you, Jake,
You're making such a big mistake.
And what is more, what makes me sore,
She forgets just what a woman's for."

"To make our teas, to chop down trees,
To scrub floors, on her hand and knees,
To fetch my dole, get in the coal,
Clean out the bloody bogie hole,
To wash the glass, to mow the grass,
To never let a moment pass,

In idleness, but nonetheless,
Always be neat and smart in dress,
Never lose sight, it is her right,
To work and slave, from morn to night,
To duck and dive, to graft and strive,
It makes a woman feel alive!"

"One day, Tone, you will be grown,
You'll have a woman of your own,
You think I scold, but when you're old,
Think of the tale your old dad told.
Some years ago, a bloke I know,
He was about nineteen or so,

In the hurly burly of love, a girlie,
Had got him, by the short and curly,
Love was so rare, he didn't care,
He'd found the answer to his prayer,
You can be sure, time was the cure,
Loke some old trout, he took the lure.

A chance he took, was on the hook,
Was hauled out, gasping, from the brook,
Was in the net, too late to fret,
He'd diced with life and lost the bet."
I heard this folly and thought the wally
Had gone completely off his trolley.

But I kept mum, I was his son,
I listened, as he waffled on,
"This is the way that people play,
They only think about today,
Forget the cost, the dice is tossed,
Then say they're cheated when they've lost.

"So like a trout that's been hauled out,
He'd tried life's rigid rules to flout.
He saw the prize before his eyes,
And to the bait, he had to rise,
He wagered grand, on a poor hand,
And made off with his contraband."

I made pretence, in deference,
That all this rubbish made some sense,
Listened perforce, and in due course,
Dad got down off his hobby horse.
"It was a day in early May,
When my mate Jim first made his play,

Fresh flowers he bought, and came to court,
And win the sweet love that he sought,"
Sue had a hunch, she took his bunch,
And asked the poor slob in to lunch,
"I'm a good cook," He thought, "What luck!"
His lips were nibbling round the hook,

He swaggered in. She said, "Oh Jim,
Could you perhaps, take out the bin?
I'm very small, and you're so tall,
It would be no strain on you at all."
His chest swelled out. The dozy lout,
Carried her bin, (one handed) out,

He would live to rue, and curse it too,
But he said, "What else can I do,
To earn my dinner? Sue was no sinner,
But knew when she was on a winner.
Winsome and slim, she said, "Oh Jim,"
And held her soft arms out to him.

Though in a state, Jimbo, my mate,
Had grim forebodings of his fate,
But thought, "I'll pull it," He bit the bullet,
The hook was halfway down his gullet.
From that day's noon until the gloom,
Was falling, and the rising moon,

Lent its pale glow, did poor Jim mow,
And cut the hedges, dig, and hoe,
Gave up the fight with fading light,
And kissed his darling Sue goodnight,
Then staggered, beat, back up the street,
With half of her garden on his feet.

Yet by his sweat, he'd won his pet,
Though little knew just what he'd get,
Sue kept her head, it must be said,
Within two months, the two were wed.
But, woe betide, when they were tied,
A strange change overcame his bride,

For when your wife controls your life,
Her tongue gets sharper than a knife,
The more you stake, concessions make,
The more, you'll find, she wants to take.
And all too fast, the die was cast,
Jim's days of freedom all were past.

He worked, just then, from two to ten,
And then came home to start again,
She had found the slob another job,
Humping coal, for a chap named Bob.
Left on her nellie, she stuffed her belly,
And watched Australian soaps on telly,

Before Jim's eyes, to his surprise,
His Sue became a different size,
The slender Sue that he once knew,
Was fast becoming more like two.
So life grew grim for poor old Jim,
Yet he would not have given in,

But such is fate, he came home late,
Caught Sue in bed with Bob, his mate,
Jim gave a shout, bashed Bob about,
And fetched Sue a terrific clout,
His temper flares, he roars and glares,
He throws Robert straight down the stairs.

Not at his best, and hardly dressed,
Bob staggers homeward, in his vest,
Drunk as a brewer, and never bluer,
He trips, and pitches down a sewer,
Now where he goes, nobody knows,
Poetic justice I suppose,

A mucky mate he's been of late,
And mucky has been Robert's fate.
And Jim, meanwhile, his temper vile,
Has done poor Susan up in style,
She's black and blue, her shift torn through,
She's locked herself inside the loo.

Jim sods off out, barges about,
He gets himself half cut on stout,
Then, sick with pain, and in the rain,
Comes home, to start of Sue again.
She begs him, "please," Down on her knees,
"Forgive me for my trespasses."

"I've given you strife, but all my life,
I'll be a good and faithful wife."
Jim was a toff, he let her off,
And what is more, he didn't cough,
So no one knew about his Sue,
The things that she had got up to.

But from that day, it's true to say,
A new regime came into play,
Sue lost her fat, Jim saw to that,
She hardly ate, she never sat,
Jim had his say, and by the way,
Sue grew more cheerful every day.

She was a dolly, forever jolly,
And better trained than any collie,
Life was a joke for this young bloke,
She called him "Master," When she spoke,
"You see, young Ben," My dad said then,
Women just aren't the same as men.

If any fool should let them rule,
Then they'll just treat him like a tool,
They've no respect for intellect,
Some men from Mensa are henpecked,
It's alright Pete, when you first meet,
To sweep a young girl off her feet,

Take her bouquets and fondly gaze,
Flatter her in a thousand ways,
But when it's done, the race is run,
The battle for her heart is won,
Look into her eyes, and put her wise,
She needs to know how the land lies.

It's time, you see, take it from me,
To assert your authority."
My face still burned, but I was turned,
The lesson of my life was learned.
With strange delight, I saw the light,
And knew that my old dad was right.

But, foolish youth, I'd lost the truth,
Before I cut my wisdom tooth.
When I first saw sweet Sally Shaw,
A thing of beauty without flaw.
A golden queen of seventeen,
The answer to a young man's dream,

On tiny feet walked down the street,
I saw her once, and was cat's meat,
She's small and fair, bright golden hair,
Down to her dainty derriere,
Her lovely eyes, no great surprise,
Are bluer than the summer skies.

She was a treasure, I felt such pleasure,
I thought I'd die from high blood pressure,
Right then I saw I must have more,
All else in life became a bore,
I do not joke, I went for broke,
Forgot the words my old dad spoke,

Knew such excesses, I bought her dresses,
And jewelled combs for her golden tresses,
Roses in bloom, and French perfume,
A diamond that could light a room,
In such a fashion, I blew my cash on,
The darling object of my passion.

And what a dunce! I never once,
Begrudged the spending of my bunce,
Sally, you see, was all to me,
The girl was simply heavenly,
My sun and moon. But all too soon,
The song went sadly out of tune.

I asked would she stay in with me,
And watch the soccer on TV,
I could not lie, I told her why,
My bank account was running dry.
She said, "What for? You're such a bore,
I never knew you were so poor."

I could not refuse her, I feared I'd lose her,
I took her to the local boozer,
Where I was the victim of a trick,
Which very nearly made me sick,
Once in the bar, she said, "Oh Dar,
I left my bag out in the car."

I came back in, stupid as sin,
In time to take my medicine,
The bitter pill that made me ill,
Was Mrs Fletcher's son, Big Bill,
He wore a leer, was guzzling beer,
And squeezing my sweet Sally's rear,

Telling her lies, and making eyes,
I felt my gorge begin to rise,
Felt cold with fear as I drew near,
He whispered something in her ear,
And to my surprise, her big blue eyes,
Gazed up, into this other guy's

Feeling too weak to even speak,
I gave big Billy's arm a tweak,
It spilt his beer, I saw him sneer,
"Some clumsy buggers come in here."
A big arm, bare, except for hair,
Came whistling through the smoky air.

It landed, smack! And knocked me back,
I went down like an empty sack,
And yet I knew, as back I flew,
The strangest sense of de-ja-vu,
And as I floundered to the ground
Dad's voice reverberated round,

Inside my head, "My son," It said,
"Don't ever be by woman led,
Heed your adviser, you idolise her,
But you'll end up in the fertilizer,
As this refrain rang through my brain,
I thought I was back home again.

But then I stirred, my vision blurred,
I stared up, at the massive turd,
Who'd punched my head." Right, you," I said,
"You'll spend the next few weeks in bed."
I felt quite numb, his time had come,
He had fondled darling Sally's bum,

And for his gall, he'd have to fall,
I bounced the bugger off the wall,
And Billy Fletcher, the would-be lecher,
Was carried out upon a stretcher,
In sweet repose, quite comatose,
A few less teeth, a lot more nose.

My love stood there, her eyes so rare,
Fixed in a cold and baleful stare.
As our eyes met, I said, "Now pet,
I hate to see you so upset,"
"As well you might," she said with spite,
I don't go out with men who fight."

I was incensed, "Talk bloody sense,
Haven't you heard of self-defence?"
When she said, "Stan, Bill is my man,"
I saw that it had hit the fan.
Goodbye romance. No backward glance,
She left, in Billy's ambulance.

To watch her go was such a blow,
I never ever felt so low,
When you've been cheated, you're so defeated,
Your very life-force is depleted,
The tears I shed, my aching head,
I thought I would be better dead.

The dull days, blending to nights unending,
I mooched around the town, pretending,
At the disco rally, or the bowling alley,
I may once again meet up with Sally.
That's how I met my Juliette,
She's brown-eyed, slender, and brunette,

She's elfin faced, she's pure and chaste,
She does not have expensive tastes.
She would never go off with some Joe,
Like other scrubbers that I know,
For glory be, she set me free,
She thinks the sun shines out of me.

All the expense, the vile torments,
I put down to experience,
For as you see, it proved to me,
The truth of Dad's philosophy.
I don't feel blue, I feel brand new,
Sally is just someone I once knew.

Met her one night, she looked a fright,
She'd felt the force of Billy's right.
When Bill gets high, fists tend to fly,
He'd very often black her eye.
He came in then, and that was when,
I duffed the bugger up again!

Not from heartache, make no mistake,
I did it just for old time's sake.
Then headed for the "Her indoors",
Who is worth a million Sally Shaws.
My name is Stan, and I'm a man,
Who'll never be an also-ran.

Infinity, Eternity, Time,
Space, and other stuff.

Infinity, a word defining not what is, but what is not,
Numberless, endless, past divining, exactly where?
precisely what?
Your Starcraft travels on and on, beyond the stars,
On, through a billion lifetimes, you, that billionth man,
Are bound to find, infinity, is just as far,
As when your distant ancestor, long dead, began,
The voyage. You may say that simply cannot be,
"Take a lot away from more, you're left with less," you
scoff,
But without limit, beyond measure, that's infinity,
Or, put another way, Its' quite a long way off.

Another craft is on a routine trip to Mars.
The accelerator jams on the way home. That's bad!
 Far worse than the same problem in your family car.
 It means you're back, before you leave the launching
pad.
Though actually, the speed of light. (They say)
 Is a constant nothing ever can exceed.
And to the nearest star, four million million K's.
But wormholes lurk out there, (They can't be seen)
They work (Wake up!)) by simply Folding space.
And can take you there in less time than it takes,
To say, across the awesome vastness of the void

An atom! The smallest structure to exist?
Well no, it's made from other, smaller things.
Much smaller things,(They're easily missed)
And they're jigging around a nucleus, I think,
Spinning like Morris Dancers, at a country fair,
So they must be the smallest things? Except for Quarks!
So small, we can't be sure they're even there.
But could be made, or not, of even smaller things,
Wait a second though, that makes me think,

There was no space, no time, in fact, sod all,
But compressed within the tiny boundaries
Of a speck of stuff, immeasurably small,
Was the mass of everything that was to be,
A mass so great, so small, it must implode,
And in that instant, time and space were born,
Planets and suns have spewed into the void,
For fourteen billion years, but will return,
From whence they came, then time itself will end,

Hold on! Let's not forget, we have eternity,
Another simple concept, which defeats the mind,
Though many may say they understand it well,
It means there's no beginning, and no end to time,
Our ears receive the message, but our brains rebel,
Before our little births, before the birth of stars,
Eons before the forming of the Milky Way,
Time was, before the Big Bang, there was something
more,

And something more when all the stars have burned away.

When we, and all we'll ever know, are gone to dust,
Still time will flow serenely on. All this I know.
Much wiser men than I can be, have said I must,
Believe, why not believe? It may be so.
Or is the big old fellow, with a beard of white,
Who made the lot, just for a bit of fun,
Laughing out there somewhere, on a cloud tonight?
Enjoying a cup of coffee, and a bun.

A woman's place,

I met a man I work with,
He was drinking in the public bar,
And chatting up the barmaid,
Well, he has an easy way with him,
He bought me and her a drink,
And bought another bloke he knew a jar,
I said I'd seen him somewhere,
The night before, he gave a tipsy grin,

"Everybody's got to be somewhere, mate,
On Mondays I drink at the Swan,
Tuesdays, I'm in the Lion, am I?
Oh yes, or in the Railway Inn,
Wednesdays and Thursdays, where?
Yeh, I'm usually in The Rising Sun,
The Duke of York on Fridays,
Well, unless he's got a pop group in.

Then I go to the Miner's Arms,
Either that, or to the Jug O Foam,
Saturday, it's the Ring O Bells,
Or else that glitzy modern pub,
That's if I'm not off with my mates,
Watching the Wolves lose at home,
Then we all drink in Wolverhampton,
Sunday nights, I go down the club,"

"What does your wife do?" "Do?" He said,
"We've got two kids, what do you think,
I tell you mate, she loves it,
When I'm out, she gets some sewing done,
She runs up all our curtains, bedspreads,
It's enough to drive a man to drink,"
He laughed, "She's always on the go,
I think it's her idea of fun."

I didn't see him for a month,
But when I did, man, was he drunk,
Clutching a half- drunk glass of Scotch,
His face was like a wet weekend,
He didn't look the same somehow,
I got the feeling that he'd shrunk,
I said, "You're looking rough,",
He said, "Oh yeah, tell me about it, friend,"

"She's done the dirty on me pal,
Would you believe? With my best mate,
I thought I'd go home early,
There was a good match on the box,
Well, the kids are at her mother's,
She's on the mat, in a right bloody state,
So while I'm getting pissed,
That bastard's getting off his rocks."

"It turns my guts." I said "Sorry mate,
That's tough, but what did you expect?"
He sobered for a second,
And I thought he looked belligerent,
But then he sighed, and shook his head,
"Bloody women you know, my life is wrecked,
You can't trust the bitches mate, no way,"
He just had no idea what I meant.

The voice of experience.

When I was young, and didn't have a clue,
Stumbling into the mire, at every turn,
Gran told me what I should, and shouldn't do,
"You play with fire, young man, you will get burned,
When Gran was not around, to put me straight,
Granddad was there, with hair semi -detached,
"Can't have your cake and eat it," He would state,
And,"Never count your chickens, till they're hatched."

My uncle Jack was wisest of them all,
Everyone said, "Our Jack? One of the best,"
But Jack would say, "Pride goes before a fall."
"There's many a true word spoken in jest."
My old dad, too, was one of my advisers,
"More haste less speed," He'd tell me, with a grin,
"Time flies," He'd say, "So spend it like a miser,"
"And every game you play son, play to win."

Mum said "There's just one king for every kingdom,
Many a slip, my lad, twixt cup and lip.
A little knowledge is a dangerous thing, son,
For in some ways, life is just a lucky dip."
"Don't rush your fences. Patience is a virtue,"
Said Auntie Flo, "Always remember this,
What you don't know, my boy, can never hurt you,
For in the end, son, ignorance is bliss."

My school days done at last, and in the work- place,
My boss was always ready with advice,
"Time is money," He would say, "But haste makes waste,"
"You can only cut once, so measure twice."
"A wise man reads the map before the trip,"
"The fastest doesn't always win the race,"
"A haporth less of tar can spoil the ship"
And, "Don't cut off your nose to spite your face."

And when I met the girl who I would wed,
"A faithful heart," Said Mum, "Is more than treasure."
Dad said, "The heart must never rule the head,"
"Marry in haste," Said Jack, "Repent at leisure."
Gran said, "Beware, when passion rules the roost.
You'll find that common sense has fled the nest,"
Granddad said, "Sauce for gander, sauce for goose."
"You've found the best," Said Auntie Flo, "Forget the rest."

But now, I am as old as they were then,
The fires of youth, have dwindled to an ember,
I can enrich the minds of younger men,
Pass on all the wise words that I remember,
But they listen, with a condescending smile,
And give my words of wisdom the cold shoulder,
You can't fool all the people, all the while,
They know that I'm not wiser, only older.

Bad Dads. (2)

The devil's Advo-cate.

A boy, they say, to find his way,
In this life, must have, every day,
Love on demand, a guiding hand,
From parents, who will understand,
His every need, nourish and feed,
That was no part of my dad's creed!

If I went wrong when I was young,
I got the rough edge of his tongue.
A communist, a pragmatist,
But most of all, an atheist,
Bolshie and mad, that was my dad,
Folks said, yet he was not all bad.

What I relate will illustrate,
That in some ways, the man was great.
It's best if I begin my lie,
When I was just about knee-high,
We had a hound, one I had found,
If dad was asked to spend a pound,

On any pet, he'd get upset,
And break out in a clammy sweat.
But Mick was free. My dad said, "He,
Seems like the perfect pet to me."
Just for a joke, the charming bloke,
Trained Mick to bite religious folk,

The sight, to me, was strange to see,
He'd hide, disguised, behind a tree,
Give a fearsome cry as Mick went by,
The poor old dog would nearly die.
Or, (This is sick) creep up on Mick,
And poke him, with a sharpened stick.

When his evil mission came to fruition,
It was not unlike nuclear fission.
The dog was goaded, patience eroded,
Until one day, he just exploded!
His first attacks, to state the facts,
On peddlers of religious tracts,

Were a grim sight. They came one night,
Radiant with sweetness and with light,
By heaven blessed with holy zest,
Mickey, I fear, was not impressed.
They saw the cur, all teeth and fur,
And arms and legs became a blur,

No airs and graces, with ashen faces,
They headed for wide open spaces,
At speed they went, keen to prevent,
Mick pressing home his argument.
Mick was upset, he became quite petty,
And tore their "War Cries," To confetti,

My dad was glad when Mick went mad,
"I don't think it's a passing fad,"
He said, "No doubt, what Mick's about,
Is keeping bible bashers out."
And then, one day, I'm sad to say,
The vicar called, to point the way,

The golden view, the chosen few.
But Mick had his own vision too,
The holy man just turned and ran,
He sensed the dog was not a fan,
Mick was delighted, and so excited,
He grabbed the vicar's bum to bite it,

That suit, I fear, had lost its rear,
He must have felt a little queer,
My dad, the lout, just fell about,
He almost laughed his eyeballs out.
But the vicar, he showed dignity,
(And some of his anatomy)

Said to my dad, "You make me sad,
You are a bounder and a cad
The man had flair, with saintly air,
He braved the crowded thoroughfare
He was the first, the day was cursed,
And all the dog's restraints had burst,

Got so much fun from what he'd done,
He started biting everyone,
Men from the force, postmen, of course,
And once, a ragman, and his horse,
Reps carrying cases, men wearing braces,
And those with hats, or hairy faces,

But his worst intent was surely meant,
For those of a religious bent.
He'd lie in wait inside the gate,
"Old Mick, the devil's advocate."
My dad would say, that was his way,
(He says it like that, to this day.)

(If you've a mission for erudition,
Give up now! He would never listen.)
But those, in brief, who came to grief,
Suffered a crisis of belief,
Some reverted, some were converted,
But all of them were quite diverted,

Young Father Haith, strong in his faith,
Stood firm, against the white fanged wraith,
Such faith denies all compromise,
He fixed the dog with cool grey eyes,
Saying, "I reject thee, you'll not deflect me,
The holy angels will protect me,"

His voice rang clear, he knew no fear,
Mick seized the holy father's rear,
Like lightning greased. The handsome priest,
Now wears the foul mark of the Beast,
By night, unfrocks (Except for socks)
Ram 's horns, and long black flowing locks,

He worships the dread entity,
And with the local girls, makes free,
In ritual dire, and wild desire,
Risks his dark lord's eternal fire.
While a Mormon wight Mick put to flight,
Became a witness, overnight,

Was sadly caught, redress was sought,
He took Dad, and the dog to court,
Old Mick's defence cost fifty pence,
It was the signs from off our fence,
And off our gate. The magistrate,
Said "You were warned, but would tempt fate."

The court was smitten by what was written,
"Keep out, trespassers will be bitten."
So Mick, set free, repeatedly,
Made his mark on theology,
Dad watched at leisure, convulsed with pleasure,
And a delight to great to measure,

He has a phrase, "Those were the days,"
And every time, his eyes will glaze.
Mick was his friend, but all roads bend,
And all good things come to an end,
The dog was old, no longer bold,
One day, into a ditch he rolled,

And there did lie, with glassy eye,
And stiff legs pointing to the sky.
Dad gave groan, a long-drawn moan,
Was shaken to the very bone,
The poor old dog lay like a log,
I thought my dad would slip a cog,

And from that day, it's strange to say,
His hair turned absolutely grey,
And what is more, the mean old boor,
Grew even meaner than before,
He was obsessed, a man possessed,
Until he'd laid the dog to rest,

He worked alone, a cairn of stones,
Raised over the old warrior's bones,
And at his head, carved in Dad's shed,
An epitaph, which simply said,
In copperplate, "Here lies my mate,
Old Mick, the Devil's advocate."

Confessions of an addict.

I fear I'm not as other men,
For when I love, I am snowed under,
I go to sleep in torment, then,
Wake up next morning, filled with wonder,
For most men, love's well down the list,
About fourth, in the batting order,
Behind mates, football, getting pissed,
Though they'll give what they can afford,

A small donation, once a week,
To love,(Some call it charity),
Maybe I'm just some sort of freak,
But that would never do for me.
I'll not go far for fame or wealth,
But where love leads, I have to follow,
I lose the plot, immerse myself,
Like an old boar, in his favourite wallow.

I love the sound of women's voices,
Don't give a bugger what they say,
When I hear her speak, my heart rejoices,
And she can prattle on all day.
That gentle song, sweeter than birds,
More restful than a chuckling stream,
Brings me such peace, torrents of words,
Over and round me, like a dream.

She's more than life to me, believe me,
She's my confidant, my wife and lover,
I know for sure, if she should leave me,
I'll never ever find another.

The learning curve.

Some people think, 'cos I'm a bouncer,
I must be the kind of chap,
Who simply can't have "Tender feelings,"
For his bit of stuff. What crap!
I've got nice feelings for my bint,
Feelings as nice as any vicar's,
I want to get into her head,
You know? Not just into her knickers.

Saw her in the club, one night,
Surrounded by a bunch of rockers,
And thought she was the sweetest sight,
Blonde hair, blue eyes, fantastic knockers.
And well, she just came on to me,
Like I was Tom Cruise or, I don't know,
Anyway, she was all over me,
Maybe because I had to throw,

Some ugly git out of the place,
For grabbing her backside. I think
The fool was just out of his face,
Some people just can't hold their drink,
Now on me, no effect, oh no,
I drink the stuff like it was coke!
No sweat. What was I saying, though?
Oh yes, my bint, I do not joke,

That chick in her underwear!
Man! All your birthdays come at once,
That figure, God! That long blonde hair,
Don't look at her like that, you dunce!
But as I said, that nothing, Lee,
Her brother, told her I'm a "Lout,"
With, "No concept of decency."
I ought to punch the fat sod out.

"No finer feelings," So he said,
"A monkey, in a monkey suit,"
I know she'd kick me out of bed,
Or I'd have smacked the little fruit,
But no! I'm gonna show them all,
Especially that know-all shmuck,
I'll make the little bastard crawl,
Today, I bought myself a book!

Thoughts on a Summer evening.

Thank God!
I have escaped into the garden,
Some things in life are hard to take,
How I hate the frantic, cheerful inanities,
Of game shows, canned laughter, disc jockeys,
Those modern film makers, who mistake,
Crudity, violence, and obscenity,
For realism,
 It's odd,

I do not like,
Parties, where people think,
That if you can hear each other speak,
You can not be having a good time,
Barbecues, with rock music played outside,
On Summer afternoons,
Oh, and motorbikes.

But I have to say,
That silence can be worse,
Silence can be more than just,
The absence of sound, at times,
Silence is like an empty void,
A vacuum, which, in spite of me,
My sombre thought flood out to fill,
With purple shadows, the shining days,
Slipping away, the clock, inexorably ticking,
To the last act in the play.

But life is sweet,
There is a middle ground,
The trickle and splash of bright water,
Into the pool. The aggressive singing,
Of a tiny wren, perched on the hedgerow,
Watching with you, my love, as our children play,
Laughing, unselfconsciously, their clear, unclouded eyes,
As free of care, as the spaniel,
Who lies at our feet.

On Wrekin Hill.

When gentle Spring has clothed old Wrekin's slopes
anew,
Looming blue-black, under this Winter sky,
Walk the familiar paths again, and when you do,
Perhaps you'll pause awhile, and think of days gone by,
Smile at your quiet memories, and maybe sigh,
To think of one who always loved to walk with you.

Though sometimes painful in his gait, halting and slow.
The same old winding foot-worn ways where he ran wild,
Once on a sunny time, with rustic sword and bow,
In secret glades, among the rustling trees, beguiled,
Away the dreaming hours, no scrawny urchin child,
But fearless Robin Hood, or valiant Ivanhoe.

And with the passing years, the ragged urchin grew,
Tall and strong, as weeds upon a midden grow,
Still he walked alone in Ercall woods, but thoughts of you,
Went with him always now, wherever he would go,
And bitter loneliness, only young lovers know,
That that are one alone, who would be one of two.

Until, as rumoured war, became dread certainty,
He looked into your eyes at last, was free again,
You stood on Wrekin Hill, he held you joyously,
Watching cloud shadows, drifting over fields of grain,
To Wenlock, and beyond, across the Shropshire Plain,
While sounds of distant thunder rolled across the sea.

The years of peace, slipping away like shifting sand,
Remember in those precious days, you came to know,
Walking the quiet sequestered ways, a quiet man,
Born of these hills, above the brawling Severn's flow,
Loving the land and you, knowing he had to go,
For now, the distant thunder, was a chill command.

Calling the young to arms once more, rolling away,
Like echoes of a generation lost. A sound,
Ten million muted voices, of another day,
In awful whispered warning from the cold earth,
drowned,
As headlong to sacrifice, on the old killing grounds,
Rushed their eager sons, in khaki, and in field grey.

But one man, falling in the shock of war,
To lie among the dead and dying, would not die,
Until he saw the hills of home in bloom once more,
And your loved face. Then this quiet man, who could
defy,
The madness of the guns, shrank from your pitying eye,
Knowing himself unworthy of the love he saw.

For a fever then, was in his head, an inner strife,
And spiritless he lay, a man without a goal,
From black despair, you raised him to the joy of life,
Tended his wounded body, soothed his grieving soul,
On that ancient hill, he walked again, and spirit whole,
Slept at last, in the soft arms of his gentle wife.

So when bright Spring has clothed old Wrekin's slopes anew,
In widow's weeds, under this mourning Winter sky,
Walk those familiar paths again, and when you do,
Perhaps you'll pause awhile, and think of days gone by,
Smile at your quiet memories, and maybe, sigh,
To think of one, who always loved to walk with you.

Tyrannosaurus Rex.

I am tyrannosaurus Rex,
King of all predators,
I send cold shivers down the necks,
Of other dinosaurs,
If we ever met, I'd have to say,
"Today is not your lucky day,
You need to be five miles away
That's what your legs are for."

My favourite foods? What can I say?
I'm not really sure I have one,
Most of the day, they're free to play,
While I sleep in the sun,
I'm not really choosy, truth to tell,
Skin or scales, spines or shell,
But when I go for a ramble, well,
They all go for a run.

The pterodactyls dive- bombed me,
As I lay on my back,
Thought I was sick, or dead, you see,
And they could have a crack,
I have to say, I felt no pain,
It was a quite amusing game,
I just may try that trick again,
They make a decent snack!

In my cave, one day last fall,
I was snoring fit to bust,
Vibrating rocks down off the wall,
And shaking them to dust,
A little creature scuttled in,
Opened one eye, and looked at him,
He just gave me a cheeky grin,
I don't think he was fussed.

But then, "what now?" This little thing,
No bigger than a thumb,
Came to me, with that cheeky grin,
And bit me on the bum!
Went to a corner, with his prize,
Looked up, with tiny, shiny eyes,
It was time, I knew, to put him wise,
To know his time had come.

I gave out such a mighty roar,
It made the mountain ring,
The wee beast exercised his jaw,
But didn't say a thing,
I heard his tiny molars grind,
Just chewing on his bit of rind,
I liked his cheek, and he liked mine,
What would the future bring?

I said, "How dare you bite off me,
Right here, in my own house?
He mumbled, "I was peckish, see,
You have a right to grouse,
I'm sorry, can we call a truce?
I know there's really no excuse,
Before we have been introduced,
Hello, my name is Mouse."

I was tempted to invite him in,
To lunch, to tell the truth,
But it would take fifty like him,
Just to fill my hollow tooth,
I needed nothing more to munch,
I had already had a bunch,
Of Archaeopteryx for lunch,
More, would have been uncouth.

Life sometimes, can get lonely,
When your friends are made of meat
But these days, I'm not only.
Thinking who I'd like to eat,
So when I've terrorised the rest,
I save a nice joint of the best,
For a hundred cheeky little guests,
Who share my country seat.

First Time.

Beneath a great beech, filtering in the sun,
Dappling the ground with brightness, and with shade,
Waking a gentle breeze, where there was none,
Cooling the long dark grass, where we were laid,
You kissed me back, I felt your finger's touch,
And nothing in this whole world mattered much.

A blanket, on the ground, no finer bed,
You were on fire, skirt up around your hips,
The shimmering beech leaves, whispering overhead,
And silken skin beneath my fingertips,
No gift is sweeter than this gift of lover's,
No mortal soul comes closer to another's.

Sweet moan of pain, or pleasure when you yield,
And brutal is the power that stirs my blood,
And in a pulse of time, we are revealed,
Mouth on your mouth, I feel the gathering flood,
Such kisses then, they take your breath and mine,
In the fierce and lovely shock of our first time.

Flexi Time.

How wearily time dragged along,
Until I saw your face,
That's when time got its skates on,
That's when time learned how to fly,
While I loved you, and you loved me,
This world was a shining place,
But while we were not looking darling,
How the years flew by.

And now that I'm alone, this time,
Dragging its weary feet,
Is not the fleeting time we knew,
In days of you and I,
But one day, in some sunlit garden,
You and I will meet,
And then, love of my life,
Time will stand still,
And we will fly.

No Reply.

Hello again my love, it's me,
Why didn't you return my call?
I know, I know, you're so busy,
Hardly a moment to yourself at all,
Mind you, if I fell from a cliff,
Onto the jagged rocks below,
I'd find time to send a little text,
If only just to say, "Hello,"

I mean, just how long does it take?
To say, "Hello there," or "Sleep tight,"
Maybe your battery's flat again,
Feels pretty flat to me tonight,
I guess I'm slow to read the signs,
We kid ourselves about some things,
And when the light is flashing red,
We think it has greenish tinge.

Stupidity? Well, that's a valid part,
Of a lover's personality,
I'd say in matters of the heart,
You don't want perspicacity,
You may be clever at your work,
A Mensa candidate, no less,
In love, you will become a berk,
I'm one myself, I must confess.

How can you blow so hot and cold?
One day you're loving, sweet and kind,
Next day, you'd think I'd killed your cat!
And all that's changed is passing time.
You call to say how much you care,
And can we meet tonight, in town?
But I'm the only bugger there,
You've given me the runaround.

And when I try to call you up,
Worrying that you may not be well,
Guess what! Your bloody mobile's off,
Oh wonderful, oh bloody hell!
I've started though, to see the light,
The message has just penetrated.
I'm bored with staying in at night,
Watching paint dry is overrated.

God! Have you put me to the test!
These last few weeks have been a farce,
Let's say goodbye, I think it's best,
Good luck. Oh, sod it. Kiss my arse!

Nellie Walker.

The ghost of Nellie Walker stood,
Gazing into the bright lit room,
Her bent back to the roaring wood,
A crouching shadow in the gloom,
Above, the storm clouds rolled in flood,
Shrouding the dead face of the moon,
And hid in shadows, dark as blood,
That dead face, in its tattered hood,

Replete with wine, and merry eyed,
At ease before the crackling fire,
The young Lord Routh embraced his bride,
Kissing her face with sweet desire,
While shuddering in the dark outside,
As the cold moon rode ever higher,
The pallid shade of Nellie cried,
For love, and youth, and life denied.

What horrors on the spirit weigh?
That hovers between heaven and hell,
Grieving the bitter night away,
As did the shade of little Nell,
Greyly through rides, at break of day,
To creep within the crumbling well,
To where, in broken rocks and clay,
That slender broken body lay.

Through silent woods, at year's demise,
Sweet Nell had come, cold and afraid,
The young Lord Routh, kindly and wise,
With gentle words received the maid,
"Do you always as I advise,
Faithfully serve your lord," he said,
"I know you by your honest eyes,
Your home is here, at Manor Rise."

And when the Spring was come and gone,
Master and maid, were more than friends,
With tender words, he led her on,
How easily green willow bends,
With joy she came to her Lord John,
Pledging a love that never ends,
For Nellie's heart was lost and won.

Never were summer days so long,
Never so soft, the gentle night,
To feel so free, yet to belong,
To greet each new day with delight,
"Come to me now, my precious one,"
Sighed John, "I yearn to hold you tight,
Come, lie with me, my love's so strong,
How can love such as ours be wrong?"

Surely there is no sacrifice,
True lover will not make for love,
Surely there is no vile device,
The evil soul will rise above,
No blandishments, which will entice,
The trusting, love-blind heart to move,
Profaning innocence with lies,
Sullying selfless love with vice.

Poor Nellie would have given her soul,
To please her lover and her lord,
No price too great, to reach her goal,
And he took all she could afford'
Despoiling treasures that he stole,
And even as he drained the bowl.
Taking what cannot be restored,
Scorned the broached vessel, as it poured.

She sat upon her lover's knee,
For love made gentle Nellie bold,
"My Lord, have you a kiss for me?
Today, I'm seventeen summers old,
And come the Spring, we shall be three."
But John's blue eyes were growing cold,
"I am a man who must be free,
Don't think to put your chains on me."

That dread day at the trysting gate,
She waited beneath the rowan trees,
To beg love's mercy of her mate,
And melt his heart with tearful pleas,
He came, and with him came her fate,
For lovers can turn to enemies,
And selfish love can turn to hate,
As Nellie learned; but learned too late!

As icy winds moaned down the rides,
And blustered through the evergreens,
The young Lord, and his comely bride,
Walked hand in hand, that Halloween,
To ruins beneath a steep hillside,
Where once, a handsome house had been,
There grew a mighty oak, beside,
The ancient well, where Nellie died.

Stark monument to times long gone,
The gale rose to a banshee yell,
And now, the lord John stared as one,
Who stares into the depths of Hell,
Reeling against the ancient stones,
Cried out in his despair, and fell,
To death, in crumbling rocks and bones,
And Lord Routh's time on earth was done.

But now his young wife thought to see,
As icy fingers held her fast,
Some thing, that crouched beneath the tree,
And heard it shriek upon the blast,
Which bore him to eternity,
A shrill, triumphant cry, "At last.",
And then with love, and tenderly,
"Come now, my love, and lie with me."

Evaporation.

Come to me darling, don't be shy,
I love you, and love is what we lack,
Remember, time is passing by,
And time, once gone will not come back.

This time- it's lifetime, make no mistake,
Let's call it by its proper name,
You may well think you have a lake,
Of time to use up. It's a shame,

But believe me love, it is not so,
The lake, you see, evaporates,
There's a huge hole, somewhere below,
It's running out, at such a rate.

That soon, you'll find you're left with mud,
With the odd puddle here and there,
"No swimming" signs, it is not good,
It is not nice, and it is not fair,

But darling, that's the way it is
There will be drought, for goodness' sake,
You'll find there's not a single fish,
Left to play in your little lake,

So sweetheart, please don't be a fool,
Come to me darling, let's have fun,
Before your lake becomes a pool,
Evaporating in the sun.

The Politician.

A solitary man, he walked in sorrow,
To many years of bitter winds had blown,
Brave dreams, and high ideals he'd had, to hollow,
Empty dead words, all fire and passion gone,
To cold grey ashes, and to sacrifice,
The good, the gentle things he had believed,
The intellect, those visionary eyes,
Blinded by bigotry, he was deceived,
Though in his heart, was sure this was his day,
All felt as he, he would articulate,
Their inmost dreams for them, would lead the way,
In time to come, his words would resonate.

With every Englishman whose heart was sound,
But that one burning article of faith,
Became the cross, which bore him to the ground,
Never to rise again, and like a wraith,
Would stand forever, greyly, at his side,
Deprived of fortune, he at least found fame,
For from that day, until the day he died,
"Rivers of Blood," was like a second name.
That first bold stab at greatness was his last,
Like a brave-seeming ship, her timbers rotten,
He nailed his flag too firmly to the mast,
And sank with her, as she went to the bottom.

Swamped by the storm, not one he had foretold,
Watching the lowering clouds, with jealous eyes,
A man out of his time, he was too bold,
Nobody's fool, and yet could not be wise,
No man was he, to be all things to all,
And bend to every turning of the breeze.
He held to his own vision, stand or fall,
And drank the bitter wine down to the lees,
Still marching to the beat of his own drum,
Two enemies, at least. To every friend,
To where all humankind at last, must come,
He came unbowed, undaunted to the end.

Playing let's

Let's be sneaky, let's have secrets,
Let's be like those old-time spies,
Meeting up on quiet corners,
Far away from prying eyes,
Let's take trips no one can follow,
Meet, and change to other cars,
Huddle in the darkest alcoves,
In the least frequented bars,
Let's sign in as Smith or Jackson,
To secluded hotel rooms.

Park in isolated car parks,
When the clouds obscure the moon,
Let's send each other shopping lists,
Containing coded messages,
"Sweet potatoes.," "Ripe tomatoes,"
"Full fat milk," And, "Sausages."
Let our love mature in darkness,
Like expensive vintage wine,
Let's be sneaky, let's have secrets,
Let's be lovers, love of mine.

Young Tum and the Widder.
A tale in (Watered down) dialect.

Some young 'uns cannot bear a quiet life,
They're always gambling on a game o' chance,
Or chatting up some other bugger's wife,
On the lookout for danger or romance.
I knew a young chap like that, knew him well,
My Gertie said, "That lad's blood is on the stir,"
I'd seen him changing too, a mon can tell,
Cos in them days, Tum lodged with me and her,

He said, when she brought in his plate of scoff,
(She'd done boiled taters, and a bit o' tungue,)
"I'm not really hungry," Gid a nervous loff,
And straight away, I knew summat was wrung.
He sut there mopin', lookin' out the winder,
Ar, and then I sid what he'd got in his yead,
Up the lane comes Annie, farmer Jones's widder,
When Tum sid her his face went fiery red.

He wasna reet, I'd said as much to Gertie,
He'd chucked his own ripped trousers in the bin,
He'd wesh his 'onds, ar, when they wanna dirty,
He'd even wipe his boots when he come in.
He'd started saving up his drinking money,
Then spending it on trousers, shirts an' stuff,
To wear to work. Now if that isna' funny,
I'd like to know what is. I'd had enough,

259

"Alright youth? You're off your food," I said,
"You've always been a bugger for your grub,"
He looked at me pathetic, shook 'is yead,
"George, I just dunna know mate, that's the rub,
Some days I wake up strunger than a lion,
By a'past nine, I'm weaker than a kitten,
I canna sleep, I spent last night just lyin'"
"Tum lad," I said, "No danger, you've bin smitten,

By 'er who come past, sut on that big 'oss,
I sid it on your face, but think a minute,
She canna be your wench lad, she's your boss,
Forget it youth, you'll drop yourself right in it."
O' course, he wasna listening to me,
I might as well of said it to the moon,
But even so, I never thought to see,
The things I'd towd him coming true so soon.

See, Tum was ditching in the thirty- acre,
And that owd ditch gets three parts full o' slime,
No doubt to him, it must have been a shaker,
You know, in a summer frock, that lass looks fine,
She is a buxom piece, that there's no doubt of,
She's got one of them sweet angelic faces,
The sort of shape a mon wants to ketch owd of,
She's got all the right bits, in the right places.

Tum reckons he was climbing o'er the stile,
When she comes riding, through a flock o' ship,
She sid him balanced there, gid him a smile,
And in the ditch went Tum, arse over tip,

Well, when Tum got Wum, he didn't look so posh,
Baumed in black stuff, you only sid his eyes,
We had to wash him in the water bosh,
And that was when I got my fust surprise.

He's standing there, as naked as a robin,
I'm washing him down, with the watering can,
When past she comes again sut on owd Dobbin,
Sees him, "Oh Tom," She says, "Oh you poor man."
She blushed bright red, but never looked away,
Tum covered hisself, o'course, as best he could,
"I do hope you didn't hurt yourself today,"
She says, "When you fell in that awful mud."

Then she rid off, as pretty as you please,
But poor old Tum was in a sorry state,
White as a 'snip, and shaking at the knees,
"'Old on," I says, "Just calm y'self owd mate."
But he was like a tum cat on hot bricks,
All wick, you'd see him, grinning like a fool,
Well anyroad, at the end of the wick,
We used go fishing in Hangey's pool,

But that wickend, somehow, he wanna reet,
He sut there on the bonk like wet hen,
Sut down, stood up, went box-neck o'er his feet,
And in the water Tummy went agen,
When we passed the farmhouse, out in the sun,
Annie was weeding in the flower knot,
She said, "Oh Tom, whatever have you done,"
Tummy just stood there like an owd drowned rot

"You must come in," She said, "And dry your things."
I thought, "Oh ar!" 'cos we were a'most wum,
Tum started shaking like sparrer's wing,
"You'll catch a chill," She said, "Oh Tom, do come."
I said to Gertie later on, "Owd wench,
Our Tum must o' been wet, and that's no lie,
At a'past ten this morning, he was drenched,
Its four o'clock, and still he isna dry."

It's funny how the fates can change the course,
Of a man's life, for Tum, it worked a treat,
Twice in one wick, he tumbled on his arse,
By the wickend, he'd landed on his feet.
I tell you straight, I canna understand it,
Why one man loses when another gains,
Why natures gifts are always gid back handed,
And one man's laughter is another's pain.

Nothing stands still, you may think you've found it,
Can hold it like an apple in your hand,
Next day, you cannot get your yead around it,
It's trickled through your fingers like dry sand,
Tum got Annie, and the farm, the jammy codger,
She got a better mon than the one she'd lost,
I lost my mate, my missus lost her lodger,
But we gained as well. We gained another boss!

The turning of the screw.

The year is turning Darling, what a bummer,
We're never going to make that trip to France,
You've been on that stupid course all Summer,
It seems that, once again, we've missed our chance.
Meeting for a crafty hour at lunchtime,
On that picnic site, not quite the same,
And I always say to you, "Your car or mine."
Well, the joke is wearing thin, it's such a shame.

We could be swimming off the Costa Brava,
We could be on a beach in Tenerife,
Instead, were parked next to that burned out Lada,
Sometimes I think it would a relief,
If that big sod found out. I'm only joking!
I'm equipped for loving, not for fights,
I keep seeing myself, all torn and broken,
I have visions of him punching out my lights.

I know you say he's played away for ages,
And was knocking off some scrubber all last year,
But he's the bugger love, who pays your wages,
If he found out you'd be out on your ear,
I wish it had worked out for you and me, love,
Have a good life, and baby, please don't cry,
I told you how I felt, and it was true love,
Please shred this letter Darling, and goodbye.

Jealous Woman.

Her eyes were full again, when I came in,
Of questions, that her lips will never frame,
For fear of answers, that she thinks to see in mine.
No reassurance works for her somehow,
She just has that sort of nature, I suppose,

However much I love her, I cannot dispel,
This certainty she nurses, like a favourite child,
That anytime I am out of her sight,
Some female figment of her tormented mind,
Will take the place that should be hers alone.

This jealousy, it tarnishes my love for her,
And makes rancid, the fierce pleasure,
Of my time with you.

Points of view.

If the fly said "Tweet," Was fluffy and sweet,
And a bird was a scaly thing,
Would we then detest,
The gruesome pest,
Who tore the poor fly limb from limb?

If an earth worm had big soft brown eyes
With silky lashes all around,
Would we feel disgust,
When the brutal thrush,
Dragged the worm out of the ground?

Your wife finds a spider in the bath,
"Get rid of it, please," She begs,
"Do it now," She screams,
"I shall have bad dreams,
Ugh, I can't stand all those legs."

A creepy creature, the spider is,
I think most of us would agree,
But if we had eight legs,
And lived in webs,
We'd be asking them in for tea.

Now the snail is a slimy beast, it's true,
If it went from our gardens and fields,
It would be no great wrench,
For (Except to the French)
The creatures do not appeal,

But if we slid, like a snail, on a mucus trail,
And had horns sticking out of our heads,
We'd give our favourite slugs,
Clammy kisses and hugs,
And take our pet snails to our beds.

If, when you go for the Sunday paper,
You bring a colour supplement home,
And it's stuck, like glue,
To the heel of your shoe,
You'd be entitled to a moan,

But to a dung beetle, paradise on earth,
Is a ball of elephant poo,
Nothing can match the allure,
Of a pile of manure, you see,
It's all in the point of view!

Someone's got to do it.

You won't see me with calloused hands, or broken nails,
You won't see me slumped in a chair, by the TV,
Shagged out by graft. I must admit, my lean face pales,
Beneath its golden tan, to think that could be me,
With fingers so ingrained with dirt, it won't wash off,
Or eyes bunged up from staring at computer screens,
I wear a Rolex watch, lads, I dress like a toff,
And I haven't worked a day since I was seventeen
No, I don't live off the dole, I don't transgress the law,
I never took a thing that was not freely given,
I'm salting it away, my friends, and what is more,
Doing what most men do for fun. I sleep with women.

Rich women, with time on their hands, looking for thrills,
Women who feel the best of life has passed them by,
And know there's only one thing that can cure their ills,
There for them when they call, is one big hearted guy.
I knew a window cleaner once, who did alright,
Made a good living, which is what we're all here for,
"How do you cope?" I asked, "You're terrified of heights."
"No sweat, I never go beyond the second floor."
And I was so impressed with his philosophy,
He did just what he wanted, and refused the rest,
I thought, "What's good enough for him, will do for me."
Like the man from Del Monte, I just pick the best.

I've learned a thing or two about anatomy,
And I'll pass it on to you, lads, free of charge,
Though a salmon rises to a slender bait, you'll see,
Him hang his head in sorrow, if the bait's too large,
If you saw my friends, you'd notice they're all slender
craft,
Girls who respect themselves, and earn respect from me,
I give them all the charm I have, I make them laugh,
And give my loving freely (Though it's never free)
Whatever will I do, you say, when I get old,
I've got that worked out too, nothing in life is free,
I'll find myself alone someday, nights will be cold,
When that day comes, I'll pay young girls to sleep with
me.

I once had a pet.

No wonder people love their pets,
They love you unconditionally,
Long years ago, I loved a girl,
And that's the way that she loved me,
She never ever criticized,
She never spoke a cutting word,
And when I looked into her eyes,
I saw the love there, all I heard,

From her sweet lips, was tenderness,
And kindliness, and such support,
Her voice to me was a caress,
To injure me, by deed or thought,
Was simply quite beyond her scope,
And in her gentle way she showed,
Me how to love as well, I hope,
Pay back part of the debt I owed,

And give to her a measure of,
The riches that she gave to me,
I lived with love for thirty years,
Bound by such ties, I was set free,
I knew each day she spent with me,
This was as good as it could get,
I kept and loved her tenderly,
What could I do? She was my pet,

269

Now I'm alone in this cold world,
She warmed so, when she shared my life,
How can I live, without my girl?
Where is my darling, my pet wife?

The mark of the albatross.

When I came in, the air was grim,
With portents of a fight.
Her colour high, and in her eye,
I saw a steely light,
No clinging vine, this wife of mine,
And when I think about her,
I'm tempted to beat a quick retreat,
But could I live without her?

Yes, I'm henpecked, my intellect,
Has never been incisive,
But even I saw in that eye,
a look, cold and derisive
"What's up, my dear? I said in fear,
And sank down in my seat,
Her face grew red, and what she said,
I would rather not repeat!

With many an oath, she questioned both,
My pedigree and gender,
Which was a blow, I didn't know,
What I'd done to offend her,
But when my bride's into her stride,
Her colourful invective,
Gets in the way of what she'd say,
You have to be selective.

I hated her uncalled- for slur,
On my old mum and dad,
It was not true, I'd have said so too,
But I'm not completely mad!
Then she pitched in to all my kin,
Back to Victoria's time,
At last, with shame, I heard her name,
My latest heinous crime.

"You've been to town, swaggered around,
Picked up your dole, I'll bet,
Called in, of course, at the "Flying Horse,"
You've never missed it yet.
P'raps it's a task, too much to ask,
That you'd have thought of me,
Beyond your powers to buy some flowers,
On our anniversary?

If I could, perhaps I should,
Describe my sweet Lenore,
The slender pet, who I first met,
Way back in eighty- four.
Shaped like a sack, her hair is black,
And stands up like a thistle,
She weighs around one eighty pounds,
Of muscle, bone, and gristle,

She raised an arm, I looked for harm,
Both bodily, and grievous,
But she gave a sigh, and wiped her eye,
Said, "How you men deceive us,
You promised me on bended knee,
Life with you, would be Heaven,
You useless lump, look at this dump,
This rat- hole that we live in."

"Your only knack is to get the sack,
The last time was September,
And if you've done any work since then,
I'm damned if I remember."
She has a long and cutting tongue,
And every word she'll utter,
Goers through you, like a red- hot knife,
Goes through a pound of butter.

I've had the push, the old bum's rush,
From many a place of work,
Been called a swine, a waste of time,
A dosser, and a berk,
But truth to tell, I am not well,
Not built to be a grafter,
When I told the quack this simple fact,
He doubled up with laughter.

Yet I never went till I was sent,
That is my one disclaimer,
I never leave till I receive,
The hessian container.
But then I saw I would get what for,
When suddenly distracted,
(I sensed that she was vexed with me,
Just from the way she acted.)

She stumped in gloom, across the room,
A thing of misery,
She was on fire, and all her ire,
Was taken out on me.
"Look at the goo on this window, you!"
"Yes love, you're right." I said,
"I'll get the ladder from next door,"
Yes, I know. I lost my head!

But if you're not brave, and yet still crave,
A tolerable existence,
To have your cake and eat it,
Take the line of least resistance,
So here I'm hung, perched on this rung,
I feel a little queer,
I never thought I that I'd get caught,
I could break my neck up here!

I could just sob at this lousy job,
This day has been so dreary,
As soon as I'd clean up one side,
The other side looked smeary.
But at last, I said, "I've killed it dead,"
I thought I must be dreaming,
As evening sun showed day was done,
My windows were all gleaming.

A huge bird who flew up in the blue,
I think, an albatross,
Decided to go to the loo,
Up there, in the cosmos,
It plummets down toward the ground,
From high above the trees,
Gay as a clown, it spins around,
Sky- diving through the breeze,

There was no stopping the dropping dropping,
But then, a stray gust caught it,
Fate changed its free trajectory,
And my front window bought it!
I watched it splash-down, on the glass,
And screamed in my despair,
But it dried quite smart, like modern art,
I thought ,"I'll leave it there!"

"Bird muck is not art!" Said my sweetheart,
 Called me a silly chap,
She was overwrought, I've always thought,
That modern art is crap!
But at long last, she was pleased with me,
She gave me hugs and kisses,
It's worth some sweat, if you can get,
The right side of your missus.

She could knock me flat, I'm sure of that!
The thought is not endearing,
I know I'm limp, a total wimp,
But still, one thing is cheering,
I tend to flap when in a scrap,
My cowardice inherent.
Yet I possess, though in a dress,
The ultimate deterrent.

I well recall a day last fall,
A day both dull and cold,
We were in debt, that's how you get,
When you arc on the dole,
There came a chap, who gave a rap,
Upon our old front door,
With shoulders big, face like a pig,
I knew what he'd come for.

My face was red, "I'm here," he said,
"For the payments that you've missed,
So come on, sonny, give me the money,
Or I'll give you some fist."
But then, my bride pushed me aside,
And stood there, arms akimbo,
The chap was tough, but, sure enough,
He knew this was no bimbo,

There was a fight, no pretty sight,
And when the deed was done,
The bloke was sent, quite badly bent,
Back whence he first had come.
The chap was vast, but was outclassed,
Once it had come to war,
For every hook that's in the book,
Is in her repertoire.

To be so hurt by a bit of skirt,
Was more than he could swallow,
His final crack, "I will be back."
Rang just a little hollow.
He lost his job. Sometimes he'll sob,
And tell his friends, with shock.
A story fraught, the day he fought,
Mike Tyson, in a frock!

If.

If you were a spicy pudding,
I would stir your ingredients,
If you were a lap dog,
I would teach you obedience,

If I was a ginger tom,
I'd try hard not to scratch you,
If you were a silvery fish,
You must know, I would catch you,

If we were two glistening pearls,
An oyster bed would be home for us,
Darling, if you were the world,
I'd be one of the great explorers,

If you were a birthday cake,
I would just have to be the candle,
If I was a bedroom door,
Only you could turn my handle,

If you were a spring divan,
I would turn down your covers,
But you're a woman, I'm a man,
We'll just have to be lovers.

It's over.

Goodbye sweet woman that I love,
Farewell, warm heart, that once loved me,
The ties that bound us are undone,
And in a way, we both are free.

I cannot blame you that I loved, too much,
Dreamed dreams that never could come true,
You always said, let's take it slow,
And yet I gave my heart to you.

That's the way I am, if it's a fault,
I wish to God I knew the cure,
Be sure to live life to the full,
But most of all. Love, just be sure.

Who knows?

In truth, I think I never lived in dreams,
Of some bright paradise, when life is through,
Where angels strum gold harps, by silver streams,
Feeding on nectar, and on manna dew,
Waking to golden sunshine every day,
With joy, to know, until that long day's end,

Sweet birdsong, flowers in bloom. Would bless our way,
Each kindly soul well met, a faithful friend,
Never to feel uncertainty, or fear,
Never to hurt, or make another sad,
No work, no pain, but joy from year to year,
Such perfect peace would slowly drive us mad.

The bitter sorrel lends a piquant tang,
To bland meats, the rough stone edges the blade,
Amid fierce thorns, the sweetest berries hang,
The hearth glows brighter in drab Winter's shade,
No rest compares to that which follows toil,
No ease is like the easement after pain,

How precious is a love the world could spoil.
How true the vow which could have been in vain,
The glory, and the wonder of our youth,
Is greater, that we know how soon it flies,
And we must value honesty, and truth,
The more, for living in a world of lies.

Was this foul, lovely world of fire and ice,
Earned in some lesser lifetime, who can tell?
This could be our Nirvana, Paradise,
Our Shangri La, and Purgatory, and Hell!

What is love?

Love is tactile, love is visual,
How many faceted is love.
You'll come to see, as you grow older,
The hotter love has been, the colder,
It can become, a sheet of ice,
Is warmer than a lover's eyes,
When love has gone, and someone better,
Has filled the place beneath that sweater,
Where beats the heart you thought was yours,
She will always be your friend, of course,
She hates to see you in despair,
(But hates it more if you don't care)

A woman's love, it's a complex thing,
To keep you dangling, on a string,
Adds piquancy, an added thrill,
To her new love, so if you will,
Be good enough to fall apart,
And beg her to come back, her heart,
Will overflow with tenderness,
And pity, for the wretched mess,
You have become. She will not return,
But hints she may, in time you learn,
That love can never be wise, for,
You have grown wise, and love no more.

War is over.

From steeples far and near, glad church bells rang,
Cacophonies of praise, their clamour sang
In joy, across the waking countryside,
The soldier came to elbow, bleary eyed,
Aching and cold, but suddenly, he knew,
What he would not believe before, was true.

He stood, and with the coming of the day,
Something of darkness seemed to slip away,
Leaving his loaded carbine in his roll,
He left the silent bivouac, and stole,
Through frosted grass, where fading willow trees
Whispered to him, there endless litanies.

Standing beneath the rustling trees alone,
He thought at once, of Shropshire, and of home,
Long buried hopes, visions of lasting peace,
Arose, a sandstone cottage, in the trees,
Worn by the passing years, its timbers black,
With age, yet from the crumbling chimney stack,

White smoke ascends into the lucent sky,
Drifting, and the stubbled cornfields lie,
Beside the ancient woodland, with its dark,
Rides to the hall, and to Great Haughton Park.
Guilty- sweet memories of lover's games,
A gentle, trusting soul he'd brought to shame,

And grief, the unsought joy of fatherhood,
A child he'd never known, blood of his blood,
Would know him, and would bear his name, as well,
When memories alone would be of hell,
Then a dishonoured lass would wear a ring
At last, and he'd see Shropshire, in the Spring.

A sudden movement, in the trees ahead,
Bright muzzle flashes, and the vicious lead,
Like solid, heavy punches, spun him round,
And somehow, he was sprawling on the ground,
The cheerful church bells ringing in his brain,
A creeping numbness in his limbs, no pain,

Just a great weariness, he lay at ease,
And saw, between the shivering willow trees,
Where dark birds swooped, up in the brightening sky,
He watched, until at last, his weary eyes,
Were closed, and as the morning sunshine crept,
To the hollow where he lay, the soldier slept.

The perfect angle.

Time is passing, oh so slowly,
Never slow enough for me,
I sit here, hour on peaceful hour,
Beside this rippling, shimmering pool,
I love this place! It's almost holy,
Beneath this great horse chestnut tree,
Lovelier by far, than any flower,
And yet I know, folks call me fool.

Hours before the bright sun rising,
Has driven mist ghosts from the lake,
When all this hemisphere is sleeping,
Holding fast to fantasies
I'm here, no dream of man's devising,
Comes close to this dream, wide awake.
To see the dawn in glory creeping,
And best of all, there's only me!

Later, there will be people walking,
"Any luck?" I shake my head,
I know they simply can't resist it,
But I don't look for conversation,
If I want to spend the morning talking,
I only have to stay in bed,
My missus now, she takes the biscuit,
It's her idea of recreation.

I just like my own company best,
That's not to say I don't need friends,
But I need this time, with no one near me,
Just to be here, to me that's luck,
Give me freedom, you can keep the rest.
Am I a good angler? That depends,
The fish here have no cause to fear me,
Or my rod and line, and bait. No hook!

My granddad.

My granddad was a miner,
I have pictures of his life,
Kept in a box, a biscuit tin
All faded, black and white,
A young boy in an Autumn cornfield,
Sitting on the sheaves,
In a too-big hat and waistcoat,
And a shirt with ragged sleeves.

Here's one, perched on a Shire horse,
Long shorts, boots, and grubby knees,
Down a rutted farm track,
Under the wind- blown trees,
Here's one of him, a young man,
Laughing on a sun-bright lawn,
His arm around a fair- haired girl,
Long dead when I was born.

Here he is at the pithead,
White teeth in a black-faced grin,
Black boots, black shirt, black head to toe,
Black as bloody sin.
There he stands, a mighty man,
A miner in his prime,
His uniform, primeval dust,
Formed at the dawn of time.

The pit-head baths would get you clean,
You could change black shirts for white,
But inside, where the dust had been,
Was blacker than the night.
But he loved his sport, did granddad,
Played for Dawley Rovers, on the wing,
And three times miner's champion,
Here's one of him, in the ring.

Oh, and here's one of him and Gran,
When the two of them were young,
On a sunny day in Morecambe Bay,
(I think. I could be wrong.}
Back then, he always loved to sing,
When the working day was done,
Lead tenor in the choir for years,
Until his voice was gone.

But granddad's pride still kept him strong,
No one ever saw him bend,
But he breathed the dust for far too long,
And it gets you in the end.
Here's one of him I took last year,
Sitting in his favourite chair,
A little, crumpled, grey old man,
Who breathed from bottled air.

We took him down a rutted track,
And a ruined cottage loomed,
In a space between tall hedgerows,
Where a garden once had bloomed,
It may have been a fitting end,
For all we had that day,
Was a little gourd of dry old dust,
And the wind blew it away.

Sod this for a game.

"Boys," said Tommy,
"I hate those bad boys, Mommy,
They never ever want to play,
I'll bash them all one day."
He picked his nose morosely.

"Dances," said Tom,
"You know I hate dances Mom,
The girls always make a fool of me.
They'll be sorry one day, you'll see."
He belched, loudly.

"Kids," said Tom to his wife,
"The little buggers are ruining my life,
Squalling half the bloody night,
Turning the bloody house into shite,"
He scratched his armpit.

"Music," said Dad to the kids,
"I hate bloody pop music, always did,
Knocks all your bloody sense out,
Turn it off, or would you like a clout."
He turned to the fire to spit.

"Family gatherings!" Said Granddad,
I bloody hate them, makes me bad,
All turning up in their flashy cars,
Showing off how bloody clever they are."
He broke wind, noisily.

"Silence," said the old man to himself,
"Old, sick, and left on the bloody shelf,
Those kids of mine are selfish sods,
Don't give at toss for me. Oh God!"
He died, quietly.

In parenthesis.

No perfumed notes, no flowers, no chocolates,
No meals by candle- light, no piquant wine,
No dreams, no promises of future bliss,
No thoughts of hearts entwined, or true soul mates,
No "I will love you to the end of time."
Only our need and hunger in that kiss.

Like two Neanderthals in ancient days,
Long before conventions of our gentler age,
We came together, two consuming flames,
That burn to fever heat, and burn away,
Sometimes it can take you like a rage,
Yet we hardly knew each other's names.

And though we shall remember for a while,
There are no tears, we part without regret
A moment, gone as soon as it arrives,
A final gentle kiss a parting smile,
As we head out to our cars, "So glad we met
"Goodbye then, love, take care." Back to our lives.

One man and his god.

I know a man who had a dog,
A pretty pup, bought from the pound,
Tom set himself to train the hound,
"He'll be a credit, sure enough,
For after all, I know my stuff."

He took the puppy home that day,
And introduced him to the cat,
Who didn't like him much, and spat,
When the wee fellow tried to play,
Said Tom, "I know of what I speak,
They'll be firm friends within a week."

As usual, he hit the mark,
The two were found within two days,
Lying like lovers in embrace,
Cuddled together in the dark,
Tom said, "He's settled down for sure,
Now he must learn, my word is law."

As I recall, some months went by,
Before I saw old Tom again,
He carried a thin willow cane,
Which he would smack against his thigh,
Said, "I don't really hurt him mind,
I'm only cruel to be kind."

He called. At once the dog arose,
And came, submissive, to his feet,
Tom took a little piece of meat,
And balanced it on Fido's nose,
The dog just froze. When Tom said, "Right."
Swallowed the morsel in one bite.

Tom showed me what the dog could do,
And Fido leapt to his command,
"He has the run of all my land,
And guards it from intruders too,
That dog would give his life. You see,
The animal just worships me."

Tom said to me, "I do not jest,
He understands my every word,
Last night, a new idea occurred,
I'm going to put him to the test,
Clamp my camcorder to a tree,
And let the guinea-pig run free."

"They know they must not harm the beast,
I've told them many times before,
We'll go to town, you can be sure,
The cavy won't become a feast,
This little test I have devised,
Will prove how much I'm idolised."

The big cat lay, and licked her paws,
Watching the cavy in the sun,
And when in fear, it tried to run,
She leapt, a thing of teeth and claws,
And as it screamed its life away,
Fido joined in the savage play,

When Tom returned, they slunk away,
He saw the carcass on the lawn,
Screamed, "You'll be sorry you were born,
Or ever saw the light of day!
I never saw him so incensed,
He threw them both over the fence.

He bought a huge Rottweiler dog,
To guard the boundaries of his land,
Bluey and Fido were both banned,
They're out there starving, in the fog,
Tom's a hard, unforgiving sod,
But made in image of his god.

Aim low.

In the teeming billions of souls unheard,
In this world, just a tiny few stand proud,
Towering head and shoulders from the herd,
Well known faces in the faceless crowd,
What wondrous gifts have lifted them so high?

Well, most, can you believe? Have won it all,
From excellence in the games they like to play,
You must have seen one who can whack a ball,
To land at least two hundred yards away.
In living rooms around the world, we see it fly,

Roll slowly, fifteen feet or more, and stop,
Against the flag, and then, don't ask me why,
Nuzzle gently up to the pole- and drop,
"Says Peter, "Quite a trick, you can't deny,
It's the sort of thing this man was born to do."

And how casually he performs his trick,
Stands grinning smugly, in his tartan trews,
With a metal club someone screwed to a stick,
"Eagle," His face is up there on the news,
What a man," The pundits say, "One of the few!"

There are others, I'm sure you know their names,
Who have amassed a formidable packet,
Have found their niche in life, their day of fame,
By the cute and cunning way they wield a racquet,
How they play their game with strategy and guile,

Sneaking the ball past the other famous bloke,
Sweating and struggling on the other side,
Breaking his pounding heart with every stroke,
While spreading their own fame far and wide.
And adding another zero to their pile.

One I have seen, can kick a ball, just right,
To go exactly where he wants, it seems,
Rich men will raid their piggy banks and fight,
To get the budding genius in their teams,
To them, in fact, it's only pocket change.

They'll happily pay the lad an awesome pile,
Each week, to kick their balls about the field,
The spotlight shines of course, and in a while,
The rich and famous boy will be revealed,
In talent he has shown for other games.

Men of the press, as they do, will follow avidly,
In their endless quest for honesty and truth,
And deeply shocked, report to you and me,
All the naughty off- pitch antics of the youth.
And the "Party girls," who have a tale to tell.

Some famous faces have won the nation's hearts,
By punching other famous faces round the ring,
While other poor pathetic little farts,
Are convinced they're halfway there if they can sing,
(Some of them can strum three chords as well)

One chap, (He will be famous in the end,)
Paints powerful pictures on other people's walls,
Yet strange to say, so far, he's bucked the trend,
For no one has ever seen his face at all.
Banksy, we love you, man of mystery.

Once, hopeful girls would nurse within their breasts,
A dream of fortune they called Hollywood,
From all around the world they came, to take the test,
The lucky ones went home before they could.
Most of the rest? Well, that's just history.

Some girls, it's true, have realised the dream,
Stalking the glitzy catwalk dressed in rags,
Made for them by another famous queen,
From bits of fishing net, and plastic bags,
While some strange chemical has fried his brain.

Wealth? No doubt it's what most of us desire,
But fame? For all the good things it can give,
Can put your backside in the line of fire,
Weird strangers know exactly where you live!
You do not want them knocking at your door!

You look for fame, to grab your fifteen minutes,
But I found another goal that works for me,
You can get there too, if your heart is in it,
Work hard and long. You'll find obscurity.
If the ones you love, love you, don't ask for more.

Indigo eyes.

When I look into those wild blue eyes,
The deepest blue I ever saw,
Then don't expect me to be wise,
Wisdom, I was never famous for,
But now I am the king of fools,
What sense I once had, starved of air,
Sinks helplessly into those pools,
And founders, gladly drowning there.

Caveat emptor, look for faults,
Blind faith, we all know, is no healer,
We learn to take a pinch of salt,
This world is full of used car dealers,
But when our eyes meet, there are no lies,
She sees into my soul with ease,
I'll take my chances, trust those eyes,
And never ask for guarantees.

It takes two.

Ricky Random has a tandem,
And he loves the sights and sounds,
With Beyonce, his fiancée,
As their four legs whizz around,

Those who pass them, don't harass them,
They take it slow, enjoy the sights,
She is a beauty blessed with booty,
Like her namesake, up in lights.

Though it's pretty gritty in the city,
In the traffic and the fumes,
They get their kicks out in the sticks,
Fields and orchards, flowers in bloom,

Rick has won medals pumping pedals,
On the track and on the road,
But it's relaxing, not so taxing,
When your darling shares the load.

They have a tent, and nights are spent,
On those secluded country sites,
While he erects, she genuflects,
Cooking supper up by lantern light.

What romance! The Tour de France!
Yellow jerseys all the way,
And guests on bikes are dressed in lycra,
To celebrate their wedding day.

On quiet byways, far from highways,
You may see them riding free,
Love and kisses, Mr and Mrs,
Soon you'll need a bike for three!

Taking care of business.

Those medium rare steaks sizzling on the plate,
In their cosy nest of mash or chips (Take your pick.)
Have made you a strong man, master of his fate,
That is, until the day they make you sick,

You propel your beefy frame to see your favourite bloke,
The butcher, who has your sausage, steak, and patties,
Parcelled and waiting, he always likes a joke,
And as you shamble homeward through the fatties,

You watch the morons with their take-aways,
And grin at what he said, "You just can't beat it,
Unless it comes in polystyrene, or plastic trays,
The buggers wouldn't know you're s'posed to eat it."

But you eat proper food, cooked to perfection,
Baked, broiled, roasted, grilled, or fried,
She has no appetite herself, but no objection,
To ensuring yours is always satisfied.

How tenderly you view her, how she tries,
Her little pipe-stem arms, stirring the stew,
While she takes care of business, and those eyes,
Those patient, placid eyes are watching you!

Baggy.

Back then, the tramps who hiked the country roads,
Were never sent in hunger from our door,
Our mother sent them, grinning, on their way,
With hot tea in bottles, hunks of bread and cheese,
Old Baggy was another one of these,
Who dropped in at our place one summer's day,
Just as the sun went down across the moor,
Turning the farmhouse window- panes to flame.

A non-descript scarred hobo, with a tail,
A shapeless thing, in mud-stained livery,
Sat in mute expectation on the yard,
"Off you go," Said Mom, "Don't look at me."
He looked up, with his near bull terrier face,
That silent pleading look dogs do so well,
Wagged his up-curling, almost Beagle tail,
"You can't stay here," She said, "Now off you go."

And with drooping ears and tail, he slunk away,
"All right, come on," Her tender heart was touched,
"Let's find you something boy, you look done in."
And the old beggar's foot was in the door.
We found his owner, "I shall put him down,"
He said, "A faithless dog's no use to me."
"Ok," Said Dad, "Where did he get those scars?"
He turned away, "I wouldn't have a clue."

I remember we were dog-less at the time,
And Baggy, (Don't know how he got that name.)
Was homeless, an unwanted vagabond,
And slotted in like fingers in a glove.
When he was washed, a process he endured,
The best that could be said was, "Now he's clean."
Yet that scarred black face still had a winsome charm,
An air, a quiet something in his eye.

He was like some ancient veteran of war,
Seeking a peaceful post to end his days,
Companions who would never make demands,
And a billet far from all that he had known,
He would come into the house, if he was called,
Then would turn, and wait to be let out again,
A pile of sacking, in an old cart shed,
Dad piled up into a corner for his bed.

An old work coat had fallen from its nail,
Was it the smell that piqued his fantasies?
Reminded him of females he had known?
We'll never know! He rolled it into a ball,
Some days, when I left for work at dawn,
He was showing his affection for his friend,
Some days, when the working day was done,
An evening matinee was under way.

And when I walked the lanes, he came along,
Head down, trotting quietly at my heels,
It was easy to forget that he was there,
He never foraged in the undergrowth,
He never even looked at other dogs,
But one day, as we passed a private drive,
A German Shepherd, baying like a wolf,
Launched himself at Baggy, primed to kill.

As they came together, Baggy rolled,
And when the big dog struggled to his feet,
The scarred black face was buried in his mane,
The hobo had the shepherd by the throat,
And pulled him down. The lazy hound,
Was gone, and in his place, a fighting dog!
The shepherd would have died there, on the stones,
That day for sure, had Baggy been alone.

He had come home at last, the summer days,
Spent drowsing like an old man, in the sun,
Five times a day, mother would cross the yard,
To bring him scraps, to pet him for a while,
When I returned one evening from my work,
He was so still, I knew that he had gone,
He lay at rest, scarred muzzle on his paws,
Baggy the warrior would fight no more.

All you need is motivation.

Up from my bed this morning, green as grass,
After crashing out last night, the worse for wear,
I stagger to the bathroom for a pee.
Rub my dry eyes, and peer into the glass,
And get the feeling someone else is there,
A frowsty tramp is looking back at me.

Hair on end, red nose, and baggy eyes,
A thing of beauty in my night attire,
Old, crumpled tee shirt, boxers at half mast,
I know my brave self-image told me lies,
Picturing that tall slim object of desire,
An air- brushed, soft- lit figment of the past.

That's when I scrub my fat face in the sink,
Brush my rough teeth, scrape at my tangled hair,
Drag my old track suit on, and wake the dog,
Who looks up at me, as if to say, "I think,
This man's a fool." I leave him lying there,
And head out into the drizzle for a jog.

Keep it dark.

We went into town,
On the day of the fair,
And all of our friends,
Were gathering there,
So, we slipped away,
To the one place I knew,
Where a boy and a girl,
Can escape from the zoo,
And add what you learn,
In the dark, from each other,
To the long list of things
You would not tell your mother.

Powder Lane.

In Powder Lane I walked, and was afraid,
Feeling the weight of centuries bear down,
On that quiet place, where in ages gone, they made,
Black powder that would hurl the fatal round,
To tear through shivered bone and yielding flesh,
I saw a field bestrewn with carrion,
England's fair youth, the bravest and the best,
Who, spirits high, so willingly had gone,

To brutal death, dying for the greater good,
I saw a handsome cavalier, his breast,
Forever stilled, bedabbled with his blood,
Graceful he lay, as one who takes his rest,
A rest well earned, for bravely, and with pride,
For God, and for his God-appointed king,
True to the cause he'd lived, with honour died,
Unfearing, knowing right is everything.

Across his form, a sturdy yeoman's arm,
Carelessly thrown, in brotherly embrace,
Shielded the fallen foe from further harm,
The sun- browned hand against that pallid face,
At peace on the green hill the yeoman lay,
His broad back still, head down upon the sward,
Where in the final madness of the day,
His blood on fire for justice, and the sword,

He bore, for God Almighty, and the right,
Of common man to freedom from the yoke,
Of monarchy. He had fallen in the bright,
Pale light of evening. As the roar and smoke,
Of battle rolled away, two who had died,
For other's dreams, half known, half understood,
At last together, on the bleak hillside,
Enriched the cold earth, with their mingled blood.

Billy's boat.

Lost in the silent wonder of a young boy's dream,
Under the drooping alders on the village green,
Little Billy's bright new boat, riding the stream,
Glides, ever faster on toward the fall,
Red paint gleams, white sails twinkle in the sun,
Buoyant as air, the little craft is borne along,
Too fast it seems, much faster than a boy can run,
And the little boat is lost beyond recall.

Over the falls, to where two brawling streams converge,
Churning white water batters all beneath the surge,
But yards downstream, see the tiny craft emerge,
Again, to breast the current like a swan.
Plunged into roaring culverts, and to light again,
Past hedge and ditch, bright cottage gardens, lashed with
rain,
Through dark and silent woods, broad fields of rippling
grain,
Lonely and free, the schooner bobs along.

Now, rolling down the valley hour by hour,
An ancient river sings its endless song of power,
And on its mighty back, as bright as any flower,
And light as cork. Bravely the boat is borne,
The night is dark. Far out upon the storm tossed deep,
Who's boom and roar would tear the very gods from
sleep,
And in a fleeting moonbeam, on a wild wave's leap,
Little Billy's boat is riding out the storm.

She can if he can.

Can a woman ever get the better of a man?
You bet she can!
Can't be the power of muscles that does it then?
No need of them.
So, its intellect, you say, the triumph of the mind?
Of womankind?
Perhaps the willingness to go the extra mile?
Excuse my smile.
Well, could it simply be the genes that form her?
Getting warmer.
You say that since man desires the female form–
Very warm.
He'll give a lot to get his hands on what she's got,
Roasting hot!

Just one day in sixty-five.

We were sixteen at the time, feeling our oats,
On the look- out for what? I'll let you guess!
We'd spent our pennies on the brand-new coats,
We'd bought on tick. "You have to look your best."
Said my mate Phil as we scraped up the fare,
We were off to Wolverhampton for the day,
Three and a penny, I remember. Pretty fair,
"Let the train take the strain," They used to say.

Our problem was, as I said at the time,
"Nothing much to do there, when you've got sod all,"
"But a better sort of nothing than we left behind,"
Said Phil, "That sort can drive you up the wall!"
For we were rich, you could say, life was fun,
Every morning filled with promise, shining bright,
Even though we knew, when the day was done,
The brightest promise often turned to shite.

But that morning, as we left the train,
I knew today would have a better end,
In the roadside litter, calling out my name,
A crumpled thing, just looking for a friend.
Was it? Yes, I bent to tie a lace,
Quickly scooped it up, and then walked on,
And who would guess, from the bland look on my face,
That a ten- bob note had found a loving home?

We mooched around the shops, I bought us fags,
A silky nylon shirt, made from the stuff,
They're using now for ten-pence Tesco bags,
Sort of see- through but for collar and cuffs,
And it clung a bit, but I knew I looked the part,
As I stuffed my boring shirt into a bin,
We drank Mackeson in the old White Hart,
Sat in a corner, trying to look eighteen.

We read old news, as we ate fish and chips,
Smoked our Park Drives, and watched the world go by,
And I bought two third- row tickets for the flicks,
For the life of me, I can't remember why,
But the two on row three were in no way surprised,
(When lovely Brigitte raised her skirt) to find,
That the French cop was keen to compromise,
That image leaves an imprint on your mind.

On the evening train back home, we joined a pair,
In a game of cards. I won, and won again,
I'd headed out with pockets full of air,
But that evening, as I got down from the train,
A pleasing load hung, cool, against my thigh.
Back at my house, and ready for my bed,
"Hello Mum", Heading up now, feeling high,
Counted my ill- gotten gains and shook my head

I scuffed my shoes and socks from weary feet,
Hung my brand-new sports coat on the rack,
"What a day," I said, "That will be hard to beat."
I'd bought a shirt, (It was sticking to my back)
Bought fish and chips, drinks and fags for us, a pair,
Of third-row seats(With popcorn) at the flicks,
Seen darling Brigitte, in her underwear,
I could sleep content - and still had seven and six!

The cricket and Albert.

"Cheep, cheep," The cricket said,
And Albert dragged hooked fingers through his hair,
Among the sparse strands, stretched across his head,
Still hanging on, still bravely clinging there,
Which everyone agreed, had been a thicket,
Before the cricket.

For years, a home from home,
Although in truth, no more than dead man's shoes,
The foundry shower block, his comfort zone,
Was a sinecure he would be loath to lose,
A refuge from the struggles of his life,
And from his wife.

At five o'clock, the day's work done.
The klaxon horn would blast out knock- off time,
Boisterous and loud, the morning shift would come,
To smear his sparkling tiles, (again) with slime,
To splash his pristine walls, (again) with scum,
And rub his soap about its hairy bum.

Albert was not enamoured of the sight,
Moaned, loud and long to any who would listen,
But allowed himself a secret grin. All right,
Within the hour, he knew, his tiles would glisten,
And before he left, a nice relaxing smoke,
"Cheep, cheep!" The cricket spoke!

Morning again. And Albert went to war,
Caustic soda, Jeyes fluid, and strong bleach,
In boiling water sloshed across the floor,
Into the drain, to his tormenter's reach,
Albert laughed, "Thank God, the bugger's dead."
"Free at last."
"Cheep, cheep," The cricket said.

And Albert slipped and fell, feet in the air,
As he kicked out at the bucket with a roar,
And sad to say, the bucket was still there,
When Albert came to earth, I'll say no more,
In the old shower block the silence crystallized,
And in the local press, a job was advertised,

It was a home from home,
Although in truth, no more than dead man's shoes,
The foundry shower block, a comfort zone,
A sinecure he would be loath to lose,
Old Ronald grinned, and shook his shaggy head,
"This'll do for me."
"Cheep, cheep," The cricket said,

Religion for all.

Back in the mists of time, men of the tribe,
Built villages of sticks and mud and reeds,
Hunted their food along the riverside,
The females gathered berries, roots, and seeds,
For sure, they feared their gods, but loved them more,
For all things came from them. Each dawn they stood,
To thank the souls of those whose skins they wore,
To honour the whispering spirits of the wood,
The sacred fiery ball that brought the day,
And the sacred ground where their forefathers lay.

Ages passed, and a city built of stone,
Timeless monument to the genius of men,
Stood on the rocks, a fortress and a home,
And a temple to the gods they worshipped then,
When famine loomed, or drought withered the grain,
When crops failed, when cattle were diseased,
Starving peasants in the fields cried out for rain,
Knowing well their wilful gods must be appeased,
All came, with paeons of joy to pay their price,
And to praise the virgin dragged to sacrifice.

To see Valhalla was a fate to be desired,
To the mighty men who gave their lives to war,
Comrades consigned their bodies to the fire,
With sword in hand, no one could ask for more,
Than to meet again the heroes of their youth,
To drink with them around the crackling flames,
Tell the old tales again, to hear in sooth,
The martial songs, and play the old war games,
Carousing loud and long into the night,
Heroes all, who had lived and died in fight.

They built great monuments to their fallen lords,
On sun bleached sand they stood, in gleaming white,
To await the great man's passing. Your reward,
If you had served the Pharoah truly, was the right,
To be faithful still, forever at his side,
With his horse, his slaves, his concubines, his wife,
Dead grooms to tend his dead horse, on the ride,
To glory, and the promised afterlife,
Where Anubis, Ra, Osiris, Isis, Amon, Set, awaited,
With the great pantheon of gods created,

"Love your enemy," He had said, "Give to the poor,"
Gave his own young life beneath a blazing sun,
To redeem the sins of those who went before,
And of all the generations yet to come,
"Let those who know no sin cast the first stone,"
"Love your god with all your heart, and fear no loss."
But he had challenged men of power, and must atone,
They hung his battered body on a cross.
(A symbol worn in later times, with pride,
On the breasts of men who practiced genocide.)

But faith was strong, for faith men lived and died,
Though all worshipped the same god, some, in those
days,
Used the wrong form of words, and must be tried,
Persuaded of the error of their ways,
Proud as they were, persuasion, in the end,
Would win the day of course, they would confess,
Their heresy. Be welcomed as a friend,
To kiss the cross in sorrow, to be blessed,
Cried tears of grateful joy that they were turned,
And screamed the name of the redeemer as they burned.

Four thousand plus religions on the earth,
Eight billion souls. Some know their destiny,
Will take their true devotion through rebirth,
To the golden gardens of eternity.
Theirs is the one true god, they bless his name,
Render endless praise to him, in joyful song,
Knowing when, at last, they come to his domain,
They will rest content among that blessed throng,
Will greet again old friends they knew before,
Where hunger pain and sorrow are no more.

But now, here's the rub; If they have found the way,
If their paradise awaits when life is through,
Well, good for them! But then, what would you say?
To the countless millions whose hearts were true,
Who lived and died in faith, who are living still,
Without a shred of doubt. Their faith so strong,
Must honour the sacred mandates, and the will,
Of their own god! Well, someone must be wrong!
If a billion happy souls have hit the mark,
Seven billion more are whistling in the dark!

Four thousand different stories. What a show!
And the only certainty we have, is, "I don't know!"

Printed in Great Britain
by Amazon

20189101R00183